OCCASIONAL PAPER 192

Macroprudential Indicators of Financial System Soundness

**By a Staff Team led by
Owen Evans, Alfredo M. Leone, Mahinder Gill, and Paul Hilbers**

**and comprising
Winfrid Blaschke, Russell Krueger, Marina Moretti,
Jun Nagayasu, Mark O'Brien, Joy ten Berge,
and DeLisle Worrell**

INTERNATIONAL MONETARY FUND
Washington DC
April 2000

Production: IMF Graphics Section
Typesetting: Alicia Etchebarne-Bourdin

Library of Congress Cataloging-in-Publication Data

Macroprudential indicators of financial system soundness / by a staff team led
by Owen Evans . . . [et al.].

    p.   cm. — (Occasional paper ; no. 192)
    Includes bibliographical references.
    ISBN 1-55775-891-3

    1. Financial institutions—Auditing. 2. Bank examination. I. Evans, Owen,
date. II. International Monetary Fund. III. Occasional paper (International
Monetary Fund); no. 192.

HF5686.F46 M333 2000
657'.8333045—dc21

00-037013
CIP

Price: US$18.00
(US$15.00 to full-time faculty members and
students at universities and colleges)

Please send orders to:
International Monetary Fund, Publication Services
700 19th Street, N.W., Washington, D.C. 20431, U.S.A.
Tel.: (202) 623-7430   Telefax: (202) 623-7201
E-mail: publications@imf.org
Internet: http://www.imf.org

recycled paper

Contents

The following symbols have been used throughout this paper:

. . .   to indicate that data are not available;

—   to indicate that the figure is zero or less than half the final digit shown, or that the item
does not exist;

–   between years or months (for example, 1998–99 or January–June) to indicate the years
or months covered, including the beginning and ending years or months;

/   between years (for example, 1998/99) to indicate a crop or fiscal (financial) year.

"Billion" means a thousand million.

Minor discrepancies between constituent figures and totals are due to rounding.

The term "country," as used in this paper, does not in all cases refer to a territorial entity that
is a state as understood by international law and practice; the term also covers some territorial entities that are not states, but for which statistical data are maintained and provided internationally on a separate and independent basis.

Preface

The international financial turmoil of the second half of the 1990s has provoked much reflection and analysis within the international community on ways to strengthen the international financial system. Together with other international organizations, national authorities, and the private sector, the IMF has been working on a series of initiatives intended to contribute to a more stable and efficient financial system, and toward better preparedness to address future systemic problems. Among these initiatives are the ongoing efforts to develop and use macroprudential indicators—defined broadly as indicators of the health and stability of financial systems. This paper aims to take stock of current knowledge in the area of macroprudential indicators—notably, analytical, identification, and measurement issues—with a view to providing reference material for national authorities, the private sector, and other users of macroprudential indicators. The paper also looks at issues related to the use of macroprudential indicators in IMF surveillance, and possible ways to encourage their dissemination through the IMF Special Data Dissemination Standard or in other ways.

The material in this paper was originally prepared for discussion at a September 1999 consultative meeting at the IMF with high-level experts from central banks, supervisory agencies, international financial institutions, academia, and the private sector. A revised paper reflecting the results of the consultative meeting was used in discussions in the IMF's Executive Board in January 2000. The final paper has further benefited from comments by Executive Directors and colleagues in the IMF.

The paper was prepared under our direction by a joint staff team led by Owen Evans, Alfredo M. Leone, Mahinder Gill, and Paul Hilbers, and consisting of Winfrid Blaschke, Russell Krueger, Marina Moretti, Jun Nagayasu, Mark O'Brien, Joy ten Berge, and DeLisle Worrell. We would like to pay a special tribute to the late Owen Evans, who together with V. Sundararajan, was a major initiator of this project. We would like to thank Helen Chin of the External Relations Department for editing and coordinating production of this Occasional Paper. The views expressed in this paper are those of IMF staff and do not necessarily reflect the views of national authorities or of IMF Executive Directors.

Carol S. Carson
Director
Statistics Department

Stefan Ingves
Director
Monetary and Exchange Affairs
Department

List of Abbreviations

BCBS	Basel Committee on Banking Supervision, BIS
BIS	Bank for International Settlements
BSC	Banking Supervision Committee, ECB
CGFS	Committee on the Global Financial System, BIS
CPSS	Committee on Payment and Settlement Systems, BIS
DSBB	Dissemination Standards Bulletin Board
ECB	European Central Bank
EMU	Economic and Monetary Union, EU
ESA95	European System of Accounts, 1995
ESCB	European System of Central Banks
EU	European Union
FDIC	Federal Deposit Insurance Corporation
FIMS	Financial Institutions Monitoring System
FSA	Financial Sector Assessment
FSAP	Financial Sector Assessment Program
FSF	Financial Stability Forum
FSSA	Financial System Stability Assessment
G–7	Group of Seven
G–10	Group of Ten
GDDS	General Data Dissemination System
GMS	Growth Management System
IAIS	International Association of Insurance Supervisors
IOSCO	International Organization of Securities Commissions
MAE	Monetary and Exchange Affairs Department, IMF
MPI	Macroprudential Indicator
MUFA	Monetary Union Financial Accounts
OCC	Office of the Comptroller of the Currency
OECD	Organization for Economic Cooperation and Development
SDDS	Special Data Dissemination Standard
SNA	System of National Accounts
SNA93	System of National Accounts, 1993
STA	Statistics Department, IMF
UBSS	Uniform Bank Surveillance System
VaR	Value at Risk

I Overview

Substantial progress has been made during recent years in forging a consensus on the importance of strengthening the architecture of the international financial system. The international community, acting through various forums, has identified a number of priorities in this work, including the need to enhance its own—and the markets'—ability to assess the strengths and vulnerabilities of financial systems, and to develop the analytical and procedural tools needed to perform this task. In particular, the importance of assessing the soundness of financial systems as part of the IMF's surveillance work was given prominence by the Group of Twenty-Two finance ministers and central bank governors in the *Report of the Working Group on Strengthening Financial Systems* in October 1998. The working group recommended that financial sector surveillance be anchored to the IMF surveillance process, with expert support from the World Bank and elsewhere. This process is now well under way as part of the joint World Bank-IMF Financial Sector Assessment Program (FSAP), and the related Financial System Stability Assessments (FSSAs).[1] The development and possible dissemination of so-called macroprudential indicators (MPIs)—defined broadly as indicators of the health and stability of financial systems—have been encouraged recently by both the Group of Seven (G–7) and the IMF Interim Committee.[2] Such indicators will be critical in producing reliable assessments of the strengths and vulnerabilities of financial systems as part of IMF surveillance, and to enhancing disclosure of key financial information to markets.

This paper aims to take stock of current knowledge in the area of MPIs—notably, analytical, identification, and measurement issues—with a view to providing reference material for national authorities, the private sector, and other users of MPIs. The paper also looks at issues related to the use of MPIs in IMF surveillance, and their dissemination either through the IMF Special Data Dissemination Standard (SDDS), or in other ways. In particular, the paper looks at:

- the MPIs that could be used most effectively by the IMF in its surveillance work under Article IV of the IMF's charter and within the framework of the FSSAs;

- the modalities and options for the compilation of such data; and

- the possible dissemination of MPIs to the public, including through the SDDS.

This paper has benefited from feedback provided during a consultative meeting on macroprudential indicators and data dissemination, which was held at IMF headquarters on September 10–11, 1999.[3] The objectives of this outreach meeting were to discuss experiences of member countries and the international community in identifying and using MPIs for analyzing financial sector soundness, and to consider possible modes of disseminating these indicators to the public. Participants in the consultative meeting included high-level experts from central banks, supervisory agencies, international financial institutions, academia, and the private sector (banks, investment funds, rating agencies). IMF management, senior staff, and representatives of the Executive Board also participated. The main conclusions of the consultative meeting are summarized in Box 1.

One difficulty with identifying MPIs for use in surveillance work is that the research conducted so far has not produced a consensus on a core set of indicators. This is, in part, because different indicators may be relevant in different circumstances. It may

---

[1]The FSAP was launched jointly with the World Bank on a pilot basis in May 1999. The program is designed to identify financial system strengths and vulnerabilities and to help develop appropriate policy responses. The FSSA reports, which focus on financial system issues of significance for macroeconomic performance and policies, are prepared on the basis of the FSAP by IMF staff for discussion in the IMF Executive Board, within the context of Article IV surveillance. In the World Bank, the FSAP reports provide the foundations for the formulation of financial sector development strategies.

[2]See United States, Department of the Treasury (1999) and International Monetary Fund (1999a)

[3]See Hilbers, Krueger, and Moretti (1999) for details.

also reflect the short time that analytical work in this area has been done. In any case, this has meant that the initial set of MPIs that the IMF is experimenting with, in its strengthened surveillance of financial sectors, has been identified as much through past experience in the field as through research.

Box 1. Main Conclusions of the Consultative Meeting on Macroprudential Indicators and Data Dissemination

The main conclusions reached by the participants of the September 1999 consultative meeting are summarized below:

Identification, Analysis, and Use of MPIs

- While work on identifying and measuring MPIs has advanced substantially in recent years, knowledge in this area is still limited and more research and analysis is needed. In particular, there is no consensus on a model for determining the vulnerability of a financial system or on a set of widely accepted MPIs.

- Prioritization among MPIs and the selection of a core set of indicators is desirable. Use of a single composite indicator, however, would be overly simplistic and could be misleading.

- Analyses of financial sector vulnerability cannot rely on quantitative indicators alone. Qualitative information on institutional circumstances, combined with informed judgment, is also essential.

- There is a need to: (1) improve the quality of accounting practices in many countries; (2) assess the health of nonbank financial institutions and of the corporate sector; (3) address the limitations of aggregating microprudential information to obtain MPIs; (4) develop benchmarks and norms for the indicators; and (5) use stress tests as part of a forward-looking approach to macroprudential analysis.

Measurement and Data Dissemination Issues

- Efforts should be directed toward a greater harmonization of MPIs in terms of coverage, periodicity, timeliness, and public access.

- No single set of MPIs is currently being disseminated by a group of countries or seen as superior to other sets.

- National authorities differ in their approaches to the dissemination of data on the financial system, and no clearly identifiable set of best practices for dissemination of MPI data has emerged. While there is a presumption that disclosure of information promotes market discipline, there remain inevitable confidentiality concerns, notably about releasing information on individual institutions.

- Given the substantial work ahead in crafting a core set of MPIs, it would be premature to include MPIs within the SDDS, though consideration should be given to how to provide national authorities with incentives to compile and disseminate MPIs.

- It would be useful to conduct a survey of national supervisors, statistical authorities, and users to evaluate prospects for compiling MPIs, in view of the complex questions raised about the scope of macroprudential work and the technical feasibility of compiling MPIs.

II Indicators for Macroprudential Surveillance

The ability to monitor financial soundness presupposes the existence of indicators that can be used as a basis for analyzing the current health and stability of the financial system. These macroprudential indicators comprise both aggregated microprudential indicators of the health of individual financial institutions, and macroeconomic variables associated with financial system soundness. Aggregated microprudential indicators are primarily contemporaneous or lagging indicators of soundness;[4] macroeconomic variables can signal imbalances that affect financial systems and are, therefore, leading indicators. Financial crises usually occur when both types of indicators point to vulnerabilities, that is, when financial institutions are weak and face macroeconomic shocks.

The indicators that are the focus of this paper are *quantitative* variables. The availability of these indicators alone is not sufficient to make an overall assessment of financial system soundness. Such assessments also depend on a broad range of elements that are not easily quantifiable. In particular, the adequacy of the institutional and regulatory frameworks governing the financial system significantly affects the system's soundness. Elements include the structure of the financial system and markets; regulations regarding accounting and other standards, and disclosure requirements; loan classification, provisioning and income recognition rules, and other prudential regulations; the quality of supervision of financial institutions; the legal infrastructure (including in the areas of bankruptcy and foreclosure); incentive structures and safety nets; and liberalization and deregulation processes.

The importance of these *qualitative* elements calls for a high degree of experience in analyzing them, and an ability to couple the analysis of MPIs with informed judgment on the adequacy of the institutional and regulatory frameworks of individual countries.[5]

Although it may be possible to develop a reasonably clear picture of these elements in a given country fairly quickly, a deeper understanding of how well the financial system actually works is generally expected to develop only after careful observation over a period of time.

Because the relevance of individual indicators may vary from country to country, MPIs cannot be used mechanically.[6] Rather, any assessment needs to be based on a comprehensive set of indicators, taking into account the overall structure and economic situation of a country and its financial system. In many instances, monitoring of indicators over time (an intertemporal comparison) can be more meaningful than comparisons across countries, due to differing accounting and prudential standards as well as differences in the structure of financial systems. Changes in regulations such as accounting and provisioning norms can, however, lead to breaks in time series.

Prudential indicators should be monitored not only for the (narrowly defined) banking system, but, if systemically relevant, for other financial institutions as well, including nonbank depository corporations (if they exist) and nondepository financial intermediaries.

A limited set of macroeconomic indicators that are considered most relevant for a particular country may be used for *stress tests*, to evaluate quantitatively the impact of large changes in those indicators on the portfolios of financial institutions, and on the aggregate solvency of the financial system. Using the IMF's macroeconomic forecasts, and observing past relationships between macroeconomic and prudential indicators, it may also be possible, to some degree, to project likely future developments in prudential indicators.

A set of indicators that the IMF has identified through its financial sector surveillance, technical assistance, and program work over the years is de-

---

[4]Observation lags should be short to allow timely monitoring. Stress testing these indicators could provide an early warning regarding vulnerabilities.

[5]The IMF's FSSAs combine the analysis of MPIs with a comprehensive review of these qualitative aspects (see Section V).

[6]For example, whereas in one country an indicator may be constructed using a narrow monetary aggregate, in another country a broad aggregate may be more meaningful.

Table 1. Summary of Macroprudential Indicators

Aggregated Microprudential Indicators	Macroeconomic Indicators

Capital adequacy
    Aggregate capital ratios
    Frequency distribution of capital ratios
	Economic growth
	    Aggregate growth rates
	    Sectoral slumps

Asset quality
    Lending institution
        Sectoral credit concentration
        Foreign currency-denominated lending
        Nonperforming loans and provisions
        Loans to loss-making public sector entities
        Risk profile of assets
        Connected lending
        Leverage ratios
	Balance of payments
	    Current account deficit
	    Foreign exchange reserve adequacy
	    External debt (including maturity structure)
	    Terms of trade
	    Composition and maturity of capital flows

Borrowing entity
        Debt-equity ratios
        Corporate profitability
        Other indicators of corporate conditions
        Household indebtedness
	Inflation
	    Volatility in inflation

Management soundness
    Expense ratios
    Earnings per employee
    Growth in the number of financial institutions
	Interest and exchange rates
	    Volatility in interest and exchange rates
	    Level of domestic real interest rates
	    Exchange rate sustainability
	    Exchange rate guarantees

Earnings and profitability
    Return on assets
    Return on equity
    Income and expense ratios
    Structural profitability indicators
	Lending and asset price booms
	    Lending booms
	    Asset price booms

Liquidity
    Central bank credit to financial institutions
    Segmentation of interbank rates
    Deposits in relation to monetary aggregates
    Loans-to-deposits ratios
    Maturity structure of assets and liabilities (liquid asset ratios)
    Measures of secondary market liquidity
	Contagion effects
	    Trade spillovers
	    Financial market correlation

Sensitivity to market risk
    Foreign exchange risk
    Interest rate risk
    Equity price risk
    Commodity price risk
	Other factors
	    Directed lending and investment
	    Government recourse to the banking system
	    Arrears in the economy

Market-based indicators
    Market prices of financial instruments, including equity
    Indicators of excess yields
    Credit ratings
    Sovereign yield spreads	

scribed in Table 1. Background is provided on MPIs that have been used for monitoring the soundness of financial systems, along with discussion of the usefulness of these indicators. The MPIs are divided into two broad categories: (1) aggregated microprudential indicators; and (2) indicators of macroeconomic developments or exogenous shocks that could affect the financial system. Table 1 provides a comprehensive listing of the MPIs identified thus far.

Aggregated Microprudential Indicators

Indicators of the current health of the financial system are primarily derived by aggregating indicators of the health of individual financial institutions. One commonly used framework for analyzing the health of individual institutions is the so-called CAMELS framework, which involves the analysis of six groups of indicators reflecting the health of financial institutions:

- *C*apital adequacy,
- *A*sset quality,
- *M*anagement soundness,
- *E*arnings,
- *L*iquidity, and
- *S*ensitivity to market risk.[7]

Indicators of market perceptions often supplement these indicators. Because the CAMELS categorization of indicators is helpful in analyzing the various possible areas of vulnerability, the discussion of systemwide indicators in this chapter follows the same structure.

Capital Adequacy Indicators

Capital adequacy and availability ultimately determine the robustness of financial institutions to shocks to their balance sheets. Thus, it is useful to track capital adequacy ratios that take into account the most important financial risks—foreign exchange, credit, and interest rate risks—including risks involved in off-balance sheet operations, such as derivative positions.[8]

Aggregate Risk-Based Capital Ratios. The most commonly used indicator in this respect is the aggregate risk-based capital ratio (the ratio of capital to risk-adjusted assets). A declining trend in this ratio may signal increased risk exposure and possible capital adequacy problems. It is possible to estimate vulnerability based on average sectorwide capital adequacy ratios, but these may be misleading under some circumstances (see Section VI). In addition to adequacy, it may also be useful to monitor indicators of capital *quality*. In many countries, bank capital consists of different elements that have varying availability and capability to absorb losses, even within the broad categories of Tier 1, Tier 2, and Tier 3 capital.[9] If these capital elements can be reported separately, they can serve as more reliable indicators of the ability of banks to withstand losses, and help in putting overall capital ratios into context.

Frequency Distribution of Capital Ratios. As an alternative to the use of aggregate capital ratios, it

may be possible to build an aggregate view based on the analysis of the capital ratios of individual institutions, or groups of selected large institutions, such as the three largest banks. It may often be useful to focus on particular subgroups such as state-owned banks and previously intervened banks. Another way of avoiding problems of aggregation is to look at the number of banks (and their market share) with risk-based capital ratios below certain thresholds, such as the minimum required under international or domestic standards.[10]

Asset Quality Indicators

The reliability of capital ratios depends on the reliability of asset quality indicators. Risks to the solvency of financial institutions often derive from impairment of assets, so it is important to monitor indicators of asset quality. First, we deal with indicators that directly reflect the current state of credit portfolios; macroeconomic indicators that indirectly impact asset quality are outlined below. Indicators of asset quality need also to take into account credit risk assumed off-balance sheet via guarantees, contingent lending arrangements, and derivatives. In some countries, trust activities and operations of offshore banks also pose significant contingent risk and the indicators should, as much as possible, reflect consolidated information. Indicators of asset quality include indicators at the level of the lending institution, and indicators at the level of the borrowing institutions.

Indicators at the Level of the Lending Institution

Sectoral Credit Concentration. A large concentration of aggregate credit in a specific economic sector or activity, especially commercial property, may signal an important vulnerability of the financial system to developments in this sector or activity. Many financial crises in the past (including the Asian crises) have been caused or amplified by downturns in particular sectors of the economy spilling over into the financial system via concentrated loan books of financial institutions. In practice, this has

---

[7]On an aggregate basis for the financial system as a whole, however, some of the indicators that are useful for individual institutions may not be applicable and meaningful. Problems of aggregation and measurement are discussed further in Section VI.

[8]Actual (observed) capital adequacy ratios are lagged indicators of banking problems—by the time capital adequacy ratios show a decline, financial institutions generally have already been experiencing serious problems.

[9]Tier 1 capital consists of permanent shareholders' equity and disclosed reserves; Tier 2 capital consists of undisclosed reserves, revaluation reserves, general provisions and loan-loss reserves, hybrid debt-equity capital instruments, and subordinated long-term debt (over five years); Tier 3 capital consists of subordinated short-term debt (over two years). See BIS (1988, 1996)

[10]The analysis of financial sector stability may sometimes require information on the condition of individual large banks because of their market power or the possibility of contagion to other firms; see, for example, Downes, Marston, and Ötker (1999). A specific problem for macroprudential analysis is how to integrate (1) microinformation on specific firms, which is highly affected by accounting and supervisory standards and the structure of the firm's global operations; (2) information on the structure of the industry (e.g., concentration, foreign ownership, public sector institutions, overconcentrated lending); and (3) national macroeconomic information. This process might involve using measures of dispersion, concentration, large-bank group analysis, or multivariate analysis.

often been the case for concentration in real estate, which can be subject to severe boom and bust price cycles. Loan concentration can be dangerous in almost any sector of the economy, however, including commodities and certain export industries.

Foreign Currency-Denominated Lending. Several financial crises have been preceded by periods of fast growth of foreign currency-denominated credit to domestic firms that frequently lacked a stable source of foreign exchange revenues.[11] These transactions shift the foreign exchange risk to final borrowers, but often imply a higher credit risk to the lenders.[12]

Nonperforming Loans. An increasing trend in the ratio of nonperforming loans to total loans signals a deterioration in the quality of credit portfolios and, consequently, in financial institutions' cash flows, net income, and solvency.[13] It is often helpful to supplement this information with information on nonperforming loans net of provisions, and on the ratio of provisions plus interest suspension on impaired loans to total loans—particularly if impaired loans have not yet been classified as nonperforming.[14] Although these indicators are primarily backward looking, reflecting past problems that have already been recognized, they can be useful indicators of the current health of the financial system, and are often used in connection with stress tests of financial institutions. Trends in nonperforming loans should be looked at in conjunction with information on recovery rates—for example, using the ratio of cash recoveries to total nonperforming loans. Such information points to the level of effort or the ability of financial institutions to cope with high nonperforming loan portfolios.

Loans Outstanding to Loss-Making Public Sector Entities (notably public enterprises or regional gov-

ernments). The presence of such loans, which are often the result of past directed lending, may also signal significant credit risk. Depending on the country, loans to loss-making public enterprises or to regional governments may not be classified as nonperforming, even though they may not be repaid on a timely basis and/or in full.

Risk Profile of Assets (ratio of risk-weighted assets to total assets by weight category). A high ratio of investment in securities with low regulatory risk weights (such as bonds issued by governments of OECD member countries) to total assets usually indicates a conservative investment policy on the part of financial institutions. At the same time, it is often a reflection of the structure of the economy, and regulatory incentives that favor government financing in particular. In some instances, however, it might be an indication of trouble at some institutions that invest in securities with low risk weights because of capital adequacy problems.[15]

Connected Lending. A high ratio of connected lending to total loans indicates a concentration of credit risk on a small number of borrowers, that is, a lack of diversification. Lending to entities that form part of the same group as the financial institution itself is common in many countries, and can be indicative of deficiencies in credit analysis. Loans to entities of the same group are often easily approved ("pocket banks"), regardless of credit quality, and problems in these entities can spill over into the financial institution.[16]

Leverage Ratios. Financial institutions' leverage—measured by the ratio of assets to capital—increases when bank assets grow at a faster rate than capital. For institutions that are primarily involved in lending activities, the ratio of loans to capital roughly approximates the leverage. It is the reverse of the capital adequacy ratio (a simplified version).[17]

Indicators at the Level of the Borrowing Entity

The quality of financial institutions' loan portfolios is directly dependent upon the financial health and profitability of the institutions' borrowers, especially the nonfinancial enterprise sector. Therefore, any analysis of asset quality needs to take into account indicators of the likelihood of borrowers to repay their loans.

---

[11]Among other factors, differential reserve requirements in some countries create incentives for foreign currency-denominated intermediation by making it relatively more competitive than intermediation denominated in domestic currency.

[12]Foreign currency-denominated lending is often measured as a percentage of total lending. Aggregate figures on foreign currency lending are usually available, but in countries where only a few institutions have access to foreign exchange, the lending patterns of these particular institutions may merit individual attention.

[13]Adequate loan classification and accounting standards are essential for the ratio of nonperforming loans to total loans to be meaningful. The utility of this ratio may also be diminished in an environment in which banks tend to roll over loans that otherwise would become nonperforming—a practice also described as "evergreening."

[14]Some countries allow the netting of the collateral value against the impaired loan in calculating the provisions for loan losses. Different rules in this respect may make cross-country comparison of provisioning data difficult. Under some circumstances, when netting is allowed, provisioning ratios may become meaningless due to difficulties with valuing and liquidating collateral (e.g., real estate collateral subsequent to a real estate bubble).

[15]One advantage of these ratios as MPIs is their easy availability from prudential returns.

[16]Even though this ratio is usually low on an aggregate basis, risk can be significant in countries with small numbers of large conglomerates.

[17]Therefore, it has similar drawbacks. Nevertheless, it can be a useful indicator where loan valuation may be regarded as adequate.

Debt-Equity Ratios. Excessive corporate borrowing has often preceded periods of financial system distress. Thus it is important to monitor nonfinancial private sector leverage.[18] Fast growth of corporate indebtedness—for example, at a rate higher than GDP growth—may be seen as a sign that banks' credit screening procedures have been relaxed. It is important to monitor if the increase in corporate indebtedness is concentrated in sectors that are particularly vulnerable to shifts in economic activity, such as real estate, or to exogenous economic shocks, such as export industries.[19]

Corporate Sector Profitability. Sharp declines in corporate sector profitability, for example, as a result of economic deceleration, may serve as a leading indicator of financial system distress.[20]

Other Indicators of Corporate Conditions. Besides debt-equity ratios, several other indicators also provide information on corporate financial vulnerability. These include cash flow-based indicators such as the interest coverage ratio (the ratio of operating income to interest expenses), and composite indicators such as the Altman's Z-score.[21] Alternative indicators that could help assess the conditions of corporations and the implications for the banking system, include delays in payments, the trend in the currentness of loans to the largest borrowers, and frequency information on application for protection from creditors.[22]

Household Indebtedness. The quality of bank portfolios also depends on the condition of borrowers from the household sector. Information on the overall level of household indebtedness is useful in this context.

Management Soundness Indicators

Sound management is key to financial institutions' performance. Indicators of the quality of management, however, are primarily applicable to individual institutions, and cannot be easily aggregated across the sector. Although aggregated indicators can be used, they are more likely to reflect financial sector structure and the country's economic situation than management quality. Although several indicators can be used as proxies for the soundness of management, such evaluation is still primarily a qualitative exercise, particularly when it comes to the evaluation of the management of operational risk, that is, the functioning of internal control systems. This being said, the following indicators are sometimes used.

Expense Ratios. A high or increasing ratio of expenses to total revenues can indicate that financial institutions may not be operating efficiently. This can be, but is not necessarily due to management deficiencies. In any case, it is likely to negatively affect profitability.

Earnings per Employee. Similarly, low or decreasing earnings per employee can reflect inefficiencies as a result of overstaffing, with similar repercussions in terms of profitability.

Expansion in the Number of Financial Institutions. Another possible ratio of management soundness is the rate of expansion in the number of banks and other financial institutions. Whereas some expansion may reflect a healthy degree of competition, too rapid a rate of expansion may indicate lax licensing requirements, unsound management, and a gap in the supervisory capacity.

Earnings and Profitability Indicators

As chronically unprofitable financial institutions risk insolvency, it is important to follow indicators of profitability. Declining trends in those indicators may signal problems regarding the profitability of financial institutions. On the other hand, unusually high profitability may be a sign of excessive risk taking. The following (aggregate) ratios can serve as indicators of current financial sector profitability.

Return on Assets. The ratio of (net) profits to average total assets is one of the most commonly used measures of profitability. The ratio can be calculated with various profit measures, for example, before or after provisions, and before or after tax charges and (net) extraordinary items.[23]

Return on Equity. The ratio of (net) profits to average capital reflects the average return investors get from holding bank capital. The ratio has to be interpreted with caution, since a high ratio may indicate both high profitability as well as low capitalization, and a low ratio can mean low profitability as well as high capitalization. The usefulness of this ratio can be enhanced by employing different measures of capital, for example Tier 1 capital only versus total capital, and different measures of profits.

---

[18]Corporate debt-equity ratios depend, in part, on countries' legal definitions of debt and equity, and, therefore, are not easily comparable across economies.

[19]Few countries have reliable disclosure laws, however, so that data on corporate debt to equity ratios may have to be obtained from bank supervisors, if they collect bank information on their clients' credit quality and on large borrowers or credit concentration, or by observing shifts in lending practices.

[20]Care should be taken to identify cyclical movements in corporate sector profitability.

[21]See the literature survey in Section III for details.

[22]The latter indicator can be influenced by the quality of bankruptcy and related legislation.

[23]For comparisons between countries, pretax profits should be used to eliminate the effects of different national taxation practices

Income and Expense Ratios. In order to get a clearer picture of the sustainability of profits, and of the extent of risk-taking by financial institutions, it is useful to look at the sources of profitability such as (net) interest income, commissions, trading and foreign exchange results, and other operating income. Similarly, expense ratios can reveal sources of profitability problems. Expense ratios can be calculated on various kinds of expenses—staff expenses, administrative expenses, and other expenses.[24] Ratios can be constructed by setting these against measures of total income and/or average total assets.

Structural Indicators. In addition to indicators of current profitability, there are a number of forward-looking indicators that are more geared toward medium- and long-term profitability. A narrow bank customer base, for example, may signal competitiveness problems of domestic institutions and their inability to foster financial deepening through a wider customer base. These problems have implications for financial system costs, margins, and profitability. The size of, and changes in interest rate spreads indicate whether institutions are operating in a favorable environment—and may signal the existence of oligopolistic financial market structures.

Liquidity Indicators

Initially solvent financial institutions may be driven toward closure because of poor management of short-term liquidity, so it is also important to monitor liquidity indicators. On the liability side, indicators should cover funding sources, including interbank and central bank credits. Liquidity indicators should also be able to capture large maturity mismatches in the largest financial institutions or in the overall financial sector.[25]

Central Bank Credit to Financial Institutions. A large increase in central bank credit to banks and other financial institutions—as a proportion of their capital or their liabilities—often reflects severe liquidity (and frequently also solvency) problems in the financial system.

Segmentation. A high dispersion in interbank rates may signal that some institutions are considered risky. Banks may also control their interbank positions by using quantitative controls, and high-risk institutions might be forced to engage in aggressive bidding for deposits. Changes in interbank credit limits or an unwillingness of some institutions to lend to other ones may indicate serious concerns. Very often, banks themselves first detect problems

as they are exposed, or potentially exposed, to troubled institutions in the interbank market.

Deposits as a Share of Monetary Aggregates. A decline in the ratio of deposits to M2, for example, may signal a loss of confidence and liquidity problems in the banking system. It could also indicate that nonbank financial institutions are more efficient in that they offer an array of other financial products, or they are acting as banks in all but in name, or they may have set up pyramid schemes.

Loans-to-Deposits Ratios. Viewed over time, the ratio of credit to total deposits (excluding interbank deposits) may give indications of the ability of the banking system to mobilize deposits to meet credit demand. A high ratio may indicate stress in the banking system and a low level of liquidity to respond to shocks.[26]

Maturity Structure of Financial Institutions' Assets and Liabilities. Indicators that reflect the maturity structure of the asset portfolio, such as the share of liquid assets to total assets (liquid asset ratio), can uncover excessive maturity mismatches and highlight a need for more careful liquidity management. A major shortening in the maturity structure of financial institutions' liabilities may imply a higher liquidity risk and could also reflect the uncertainty of depositors and other creditors on the long-term viability of the institutions.[27]

Secondary Market Liquidity. Liquid asset ratios should be seen in connection with measures of the breadth and depth of secondary markets for liquid assets, such as bid-ask spreads and turnover figures.

Sensitivity to Market Risk Indicators

Banks are increasingly involved in diversified operations, all of which involve one or more aspects of market risk. A high share of investments in volatile assets may signal a high vulnerability to fluctuations in the price of those assets. In general, the most relevant components of market risk are interest rate and foreign exchange risk, which tend to have significant impacts on financial institutions' assets and liabilities. Moreover, in some countries, banks are allowed to engage in proprietary trading in stock markets, so it is also of interest to track equity risk. Similarly, commodity risks derived from the volatility of commodity prices can be important in certain countries.[28]

---

[24]They are sometimes also used as indicators of management problems.

[25]Liquidity can change rapidly, however, requiring frequent updating of relevant indicators.

[26]In cases where liquid secondary markets exist, one could also look at the *ratio of liquid assets to total deposits.*

[27]Indicators of maturity structure should distinguish between domestic and foreign liabilities, and indicate the currency denomination of the liabilities.

[28]Most of these indicators can be extracted from prudential returns to supervisory authorities, some directly, others via the cap-

Foreign Exchange Risk. Large open foreign exchange positions (including foreign exchange maturity mismatches) and a high reliance on foreign borrowing (particularly of short-term maturity) may signal a high vulnerability of financial institutions to exchange rate swings and capital flow reversals. Indicators of foreign exchange risk, which is incurred indirectly via foreign currency-denominated credit to local borrowers (without significant foreign currency cash flow), are considered in the section on credit risk.

Interest Rate Risk. Interest rate risk is one of the most common financial risks, and virtually all financial institutions are subject to it. Even though it is considered here as a market risk indicator, interest rate risk arises from both an institution's banking book as well as from its trading book.[29]

Equity Price Risk. Financial institutions can, in many countries, incur substantial equity price risk, either by trading or investing in the stock market, or via derivatives, which exposes the institutions to the risk of stock market crashes. Indicators of equity price risk would include the absolute size of certain classes of financial institutions' investment in equities, their size in terms of various balance sheet indicators, or the capital charges allocated against equity price risk.

Commodity Price Risk. The significance of commodity price risk for financial institutions varies significantly from country to country. Although the investment of most financial institutions in commodities or commodity derivatives is small, commodity prices are typically more volatile than exchange or interest rates, and markets are often less liquid. Indicators can be constructed that are similar to those for interest rate and equity risk, by looking at the absolute size of the investment in commodities or by following a maturity ladder approach.[30]

Market-Based Indicators

Although not included in the six-group CAMELS framework, market-based assessments of the finan-

cial sector, as implied by the prices (yields) of financial instruments and the creditworthiness ratings of financial institutions and large corporations, can also be useful indicators of financial system vulnerability.

Market Prices of Financial Instruments Issued by Financial Institutions and Corporations. A decline in the stock prices of financial institutions (relative to average stock prices) may signal adverse market perceptions of the health of these institutions.[31] Similarly, one could analyze the development of yield spreads of tradable financial instruments issued by financial institutions and large corporate issuers—especially subordinated debt—to detect signs of a "flight to quality," notably on the part of investors.

Excess Yields. Yields offered by any institution (or group of institutions or market) that are significantly above others (excluding interbank deposits) may signal problems in these institutions or the existence of unsustainable schemes that would merit close examination.

Credit Ratings. A downgrade in the ratings of local financial institutions elaborated by international rating agencies may signal negative market perceptions at the international level. Credit ratings of the corporate sector can also be important, since they inform on the creditworthiness of the banks' major borrowers. As the Asian crisis has shown, ratings have not always been good indicators of vulnerability. While they are certainly helpful in establishing an overall picture of the stability of the financial system, a relatively good rating, by itself, cannot always be taken as a reliable indicator of the robustness of a country's financial system. For IMF purposes, financial strength ratings are likely to be more useful than ratings that incorporate the likelihood of government support.[32]

Market-based indicators of a country's vulnerability—such as trends in sovereign yield spreads[33] and sovereign ratings—reflect the market's assessment of the credit and foreign exchange risks asso-

---

ital charges allocated against the particular risks. For exchange-traded instruments, indicators may also be obtained from stock and derivatives exchanges, in particular, from position and margin data. See BIS (1996).

[29]Supervisors often collect information on interest rate risk from individual financial institutions. A commonly used reporting framework is one where a financial institution's interest-sensitive positions are slotted into time bands, according to the time until the next repricing. Alternatively, interest sensitivity can be determined via *duration analysis*, weighting and aggregating the durations of individual financial instruments held by a financial institution. See BIS (1997).

[30]For a description of the maturity ladder approach to measuring commodities risk, see BIS (1996).

[31]If shareholders have the perception that the government will bail out troubled financial institutions, however, this data may not adequately reflect the underlying institutional risk.

[32]See Section IV for details. For a recent analysis of rating agencies' performance, see BIS (1999c), and International Monetary Fund (1999c), Chapter V and Annex V. Since rating agencies generally have to rely on the published accounts of companies being rated, and do not have access to supervisory data, their judgments can be affected by deficiencies in accounting and provisioning standards. On the positive side, rating agencies try to take into account such deficiencies in their evaluations. They usually update their analysis more frequently than other institutions, and may be in closer and more frequent contact with market participants.

[33]Most commonly, yield spreads are benchmarked against U.S. Treasury yields, and are subdivided into credit and foreign exchange risks.

ciated with investing in a particular country. Following the Asian crisis, such indicators now increasingly include assessments of the risks posed by a weak financial system, although the weight of financial vulnerability in the composite is difficult to isolate.

Macroeconomic Factors That Impact the Financial System

The operation of a financial system is dependent on overall economic activity, and financial institutions are significantly affected by certain macroeconomic developments. Most macroeconomic indicators are normally monitored in the broader context of Article IV surveillance. Recent empirical analysis has shown that certain macroeconomic developments have often predated banking crises, which suggests that financial system stability assessments need to take into consideration the broad macroeconomic picture, particularly factors that affect the economy's vulnerability to capital flow reversals and currency crises. The following list includes a set of indicators of macroeconomic developments or exogenous shocks that could affect the financial system.

Economic Growth

Aggregate Growth Rates. Low or declining aggregate growth rates often weaken the debt-servicing capacity of domestic borrowers and contribute to increasing credit risk. Recessions have preceded many episodes of systemic financial distress.

Sectoral Slumps. A slump in the sectors where financial institutions' loans and investments are concentrated could have an immediate impact on financial system soundness. It deteriorates the quality of financial institutions' portfolios and profitability margins, and lowers their cash flow and reserves. In transition economies, these problems may also arise due to lack of progress in the restructuring of state-owned enterprises.

Balance of Payments

Current Account Deficit. A rise in the ratio of the current account deficit to GDP is generally associated with large external capital inflows that are intermediated by the domestic financial system and could facilitate asset price and credit booms. A large external current account deficit could signal vulnerability to a currency crisis with negative implications for the liquidity of the financial system, especially if the deficit is financed by short-term portfolio capital inflows. Financial crises that have immediate reper-

cussions for the financial system may happen when foreign investors consider the current account deficit unsustainably large and, hence, shift their financial investments out of the country.

Reserves and External Debt. A low ratio of international reserves (in the central bank and financial system as a whole) to short-term liabilities (domestic and foreign, public and private) is seen, particularly by investors, as a major indicator of vulnerability. Another popular indicator of reserve adequacy is gross official reserves in months of imports of goods plus services. Total external debt and its maturity structure are important indicators as well.[34]

Terms of Trade. Past experience indicates that a large deterioration in the terms of trade has been a contributing factor to banking difficulties in many countries. Small countries with high export concentration are the most vulnerable to banking crises induced by a sudden and large deterioration in the terms of trade. On the other hand, large improvements in the terms of trade have the potential of causing problems in the financial system through inflation and asset price bubbles. These impacts are exacerbated when the terms of trade improvement is transitory.

Composition and Maturity of Capital Flows. The composition of capital flows (portfolio versus direct foreign investment; official versus private; highly leveraged institutions and investment banks versus commercial banks and trade finance) may also be a good indicator of potential vulnerability. Countries are particularly vulnerable if their current account deficits are accompanied by low investment ratios, or by over-investment (low-productivity investments).

Inflation

Volatility in Inflation. Such volatility makes the accurate assessment of credit and market risks more difficult. Inflation is often positively correlated with higher relative price volatility, a factor that raises portfolio risk and erodes the financial institutions' information base for planning, investment, and credit appraisal. On the other hand, a significant and rapid reduction in the rate of inflation could lead to lower nominal income and cash flows, thereby adversely affecting the liquidity and solvency of financial institutions. In particular, in some cases banks can profit from the management of assets in a high inflation environment, and the sudden reduction of inflation exposes the weakness of their more traditional banking practices.[35] In addition, collateral

---

[34]Bussière and Mulder (1999).

[35]Bank income under high inflation is often derived from the float on payments, the inflation tax collected on nonremunerated demand deposits, and foreign exchange dealing.

value could decline below the loan amount, particularly in cases of imprudent lending (including high ratios of loan to collateral valuation) prior to the turnaround in inflation.

Interest and Exchange Rates

Volatility in Interest and Exchange Rates. The more volatile these rates are, the higher the interest rate and foreign exchange risks are for financial institutions. The vulnerability of the financial system will be higher given (1) a higher external debt burden, and (2) a higher share of foreign portfolio investments in total foreign investment. Volatility in exchange rates could cause difficulties for financial institutions because of currency mismatches between bank assets and liabilities.[36] Past experience has shown that rising international interest rates increase the vulnerability of emerging markets (and their financial systems) in three ways: through the asset substitution channel (capital outflows), through an adverse impact on the creditworthiness of emerging market borrowers, and through an exacerbation of information problems in credit markets (e.g., adverse selection). On the other hand, declining international interest rates promote capital inflows that could contribute to risky lending booms. Moreover, volatile domestic and international interest rates could have damaging effects on the financial system both directly—if banks cannot avoid taking interest rate risk—and indirectly through a deterioration of credit quality—if banks can shift interest rate risk to their customers.

Level of Domestic Real Interest Rates. Unless the economy has high growth rates, financial institutions tend to be stressed under high real interest rates. Increasing real interest rates contribute to higher nonperforming loans. On the other hand, persistent negative real interest rates could signal distortions in the financial system created by the government fixing of nominal interest rates (i.e., financial repression).

Exchange Rate Sustainability. A large real appreciation could weaken the export sector's capacity to service debt. On the other hand, a large devaluation could improve the capacity of the export sector to service its debt but, at the same time, it could weaken the debt-service capacity of non-export-related domestic borrowers. Moreover, large changes in the exchange rate could put pressure on the financial system either directly by changing

asset values, or indirectly via possible effects on the real economy.

Exchange Rate Guarantees. The existence of implicit or explicit exchange rate guarantees and inconsistencies of monetary and exchange rate policies are major contributors to volatility in capital flows and excessive foreign currency exposures.

Lending and Asset Price Booms

Lending Booms (rapid growth of the ratio of bank credit to GDP). Such booms have preceded severe financial crises. Rapid expansion in lending by financial institutions often occurs because of poor analysis of the quality of loan applications. In addition, a weak regulatory environment, including the presence of implicit or explicit public sector guarantees, could encourage excessive risk taking by individual financial institutions and contribute to risky credit expansions. Mortgage and other consumer lending and foreign currency loans have preceded recent lending booms, particularly in emerging market economies.

Asset Price Booms. Expansionary monetary policies, among other reasons, could contribute to excessive booms in the stock and real estate markets. A subsequent tightening of these policies has often led to large reductions in the value of stock and real estate and a downturn in economic activity, creating conditions for financial distress. Also, a capital market slump normally reduces financial institutions' income and the value of investment portfolios and collateral.

Contagion Effects

Since a country's financial system is linked to other countries' systems through capital market flows and bilateral trade, the occurrence of financial crises in other countries could trigger a financial crisis or distress at the domestic level.

Trade Spillovers. When a country experiences a financial crisis marked by a significant depreciation of its currency, other countries may suffer from trade spillovers owing to the improved price competitiveness of the crisis country.

Financial Markets Correlation. Contagion risk is higher for countries that have similar macroeconomic characteristics or close financial links (such as through commercial banks, capital market flows) with the country in crisis. In particular, correlation between stock market prices, exchange rates, and interest rates in different countries is often seen as an indicator of the risk of contagion.[37]

---

[36]Under fixed exchange rate regimes, by definition, volatility cannot be observed before a devaluation actually occurs, so other indicators have to be used, for example, the volume of foreign exchange intervention by the central bank.

[37]For a summary of financial contagion effects, see International Monetary Fund (1999h), p. 66.

Other Factors

Directed Lending and Investment. Portfolio restrictions channeling credit to specific activities or sectors based on nonmarket criteria often lead to the inefficient allocation of resources and negatively affect the solvency of financial institutions.

Government Recourse to the Banking System and Other Quasi-Fiscal Imbalances. For example, a sudden increase in central bank credit to the government could lead to inflationary pressures and affect the financial system.

Arrears in the Economy. The buildup of arrears could signal debt-service difficulties by the government or by private sector borrowers. These problems negatively affect the solvency and liquidity of financial institutions.

Directions for Further Work

The set of indicators identified so far for conducting macroprudential analysis is already large and will potentially increase as a result of the additional research needed in this area. In particular, the conclusions of the September 1999 consultative meeting pointed to the need for better indicators of developments in specific sectors and markets that have proven relevant in assessing financial vulnerabilities, but that have been difficult to gauge in practice. These sectors and markets include real estate, the corporate and household sectors, nonbank financial institutions, and off-balance sheet exposures of financial institutions, including institutional investors (e.g., mutual funds, pension funds, insurance companies, and hedge funds).

In parallel with the development of more comprehensive indicators, work should also be done on selecting a smaller and more manageable subset of MPIs, notably for the purposes of periodic monitoring and data dissemination. Indicators included in such a subset, or core set, of MPIs would need to be focused on core markets and institutions, based on accepted analytical relationships, comparable across countries and relevant in most circumstances (i.e., not country-specific), among other things, to permit cross-country studies.[38] Participants at the consultative meeting concluded that the research conducted so far has not produced a consensus on the composition of such a core set of indicators. A variety of different indicators appear to be relevant in different countries under different circumstances. Moreover, potential vulnerabilities may be exacerbated by country- or region-specific circumstances (including inadequate legal and financial infrastructure to absorb shocks), which a core set of quantitative indicators may not detect.

Participants at the consultative meeting also discussed the possibility of developing a composite indicator of financial system soundness. There was a general sense, however, that the complex reality of financial markets may not lend itself to being captured in such indicators. In particular, composite indicators could prove simplistic and potentially misleading, as they may conceal or misrepresent problems by offsetting positive and negative signals from different individual components.

---

[38]Particularly among academics, investment managers, and analysts participating in the consultative meeting, interest was high in indicators that would permit cross-country studies, that is, indicators that are suitable for comparative analysis.

III   Literature Survey

This chapter reviews the theoretical and empirical literature, other than work done by the IMF,[39] which would support the selection of a core set of MPIs. In general, these studies look at the features of crisis-prone systems, with a view to anticipating future crisis events. By attempting to identify leading indicators of crises, rather than contemporaneous indicators of financial soundness, much of the earlier literature did not specifically review the full range of potential MPIs. More recently, the focus of many studies has shifted toward contemporaneous indicators of financial health. No consensus has yet emerged, however, from this body of work on a set of indicators that is most relevant to assessing financial soundness, or to building effective early warning systems. The statistical significance of individual indicators is often found not to be strong, and some of the studies have produced conflicting results. This may be due to differences among crises, so that specific indicators may be more or less relevant to each case.

We present below the following:

- A brief survey of the theoretical literature on the origins of financial crises. These theoretical studies are not used to derive MPIs directly, but they underpin the empirical studies discussed in subsequent sections.

- A review of empirical evidence on macroeconomic factors that affect the health of the financial system. This literature has focused on leading indicators of financial crises.

- A review of empirical evidence on prudential factors used to assess financial soundness. These studies suggest additional variables that can be used as contemporaneous indicators.

The literature provides some empirical justification for the use of most of the variables that have been identified as macroeconomic and prudential indicators of financial soundness. The variety of specifications, time periods, and objectives of the empirical studies, however, makes it difficult to prioritize the indicators, or to eliminate any of them on the basis of empirical evidence. The empirical results represent work in progress, and serve only to confirm the potential usefulness of the indicators.

Determinants of Financial System Soundness[40]

Over the years, researchers have developed a variety of economic theories to explain soundness in financial markets. While earlier researchers relied on movements in economic fundamentals as the origin of financial distress and crisis, recent studies have highlighted the role of the information available to, and the expectations of, investors in explaining the behavior of financial markets. The rest of this section reviews the literature on banking soundness, because historically, banks have been the most important financial intermediaries.

The classic explanation for financial fragility is given by Irving Fisher (1933). He argues that fragility is closely correlated with macroeconomic cycles, and highlights, in particular, debt liquidation. A downturn triggered by over-indebtedness in the real economy requires, at some point, liquidation of this debt in order to bring the economy back to equilibrium. Debt liquidation would result in a contraction of monetary liabilities and a slowdown of velocity. These changes have several economic implications—reductions in prices, output, and market confidence, and increases in bankruptcies and unemployment. According to Fisher, therefore, financial fragility is largely based on deterioration in economic fundamentals.

Other theories highlight factors affecting depositor confidence. Diamond and Dybvig (1983) discuss the potential existence of multiple equilibria in financial markets. Banks offer a mechanism of maturity transformation whereby deposits are often lent with longer maturities. It is possible that the "good" equilibrium prevailing in normal times is not the only

---

[39]Work conducted by the IMF is the subject of Section V.

[40]Davis (1999) provided a very useful reference in writing this section.

equilibrium, and that the banking sector finds itself in a "bank run" equilibrium. Diamond and Dybvig assume that these equilibria are a function of random events known to all agents. Therefore, a bank run occurs when agents have deposited funds into a bank at a time of low probability of a bank run, and then later observe negative events that increase their anticipation of a bank run. This study points to the importance of a high level of confidence in banks as a source of banking sector stability.[41]

Some studies focus on information issues. Mishkin (1996) stresses that information asymmetries between creditors and borrowers result in an adverse selection problem.[42] Borrowers often have more information than banks on the quality of the investment they wish to finance. Creditors insure themselves against this source of uncertainty by lending only at the average rate between nonrisky and risky investments. It follows that borrowers with high-quality investments (i.e., high-return investments with low risk) pay interest rates that are higher than in the absence of asymmetric information, while those with low-quality investments pay lower rates. This can lead to a situation where high-quality investments are displaced by low-quality investments, causing deterioration in the overall quality of bank portfolios.

Guttentag and Herring (1984) extend the argument on asymmetric information to the possible practice of credit rationing. In the presence of uncertainty about the true return on investment, there may be a discrepancy between return expectations on the part of creditor and borrower. When the creditor's expected return on a project is less than the return on his alternative use of funds, the borrower may be rationed. Their argument suggests that credit rationing increases with the level of uncertainty, and thus of financial vulnerability. The introduction of a deposit insurance mechanism is often seen as one way to lessen this problem. But Keeley (1990) points out that the possible existence of moral hazard problems in a deposit insurance scheme can lead financial institutions to take more risks than they would otherwise do—borrowing at the risk-free rate (i.e., the rate on the insured deposits) and investing in riskier assets.

Recent studies point to the existence of asymmetric information in financial markets as a source of contagion of financial crises from one country to another. This is a vital concern because more countries have liberalized their markets and are now highly linked with other countries' markets. Through this channel, negative external shocks may be directly transmitted to countries that are healthy. Kodres and Pritsker (1998), for example, develop a theoretical, multiple-asset, rational expectations model of the determinants of contagion, in which adverse effects of contagion depend on the sensitivity of the affected country to common macroeconomic risks and to the level of asymmetric information prevailing in the economy. They also point out that in the presence of hedging mechanisms, contagion may occur without common macroeconomic risks in two countries if investors hedge by reducing their overall exposure to emerging markets. This seems to have been the experience of many Asian countries.

Davis (1996) argues that institutional investors may contribute to financial fragility because of principal-agent problems in the relationship between fund managers and their clients—that is, fund managers may not act to maximize the client's profits without appropriate supervision. He argues that one way to reduce the principal-agent problem is to introduce more frequent monitoring and performance evaluation systems. From the perspective of the fund manager, when strict monitoring and evaluation are in place, one way to show the quality of his management is to imitate others (the so-called herd behavior) rather than trust his own judgment, since the initial financial asset information available to him often contains elements of uncertainty. In this way then, Scharfstein and Stein (1990) says mimicking other investors is likely to maintain the manager's reputation by reducing his risk of underperformance relative to the average for the market. Therefore, an event perceived as adverse by just one investor may result in large movements in financial asset prices.

These theoretical studies have been the point of departure for much of the empirical work discussed below. Table 2 summarizes the main indicators identified in the empirical literature.

Studies of Macroeconomic Variables

Several studies of financial problems appeared in the wake of the Mexican crisis in 1994, and before the emergence of the Asian crisis in 1997.[43] These

---

[41]In addition, when a bank run occurs, the institution tries to rapidly liquidate assets to meet demand for deposit withdrawal. In these circumstances, assets are likely to be sold at a discount and the financial position of the bank may deteriorate further.

[42]For a discussion of adverse selection, see Akerlof (1970).

[43]The range of approaches is illustrated by Demirgüç-Kunt and Detragiache (1998), an econometric study of banking crises in 65 countries; Federal Reserve Bank of Kansas City (1997), conference proceedings covering a wide range of issues beyond quantitative ones, but offering comments on the importance of macroeconomic variables; Gavin and Hausmann (1996) and Rojas-Suárez and Weisbrod (1995), both on Latin America; Goldstein and Turner (1996), which contains a comprehensive survey of possible origins of banking crises in emerging countries; and Goodhart (1995), which focuses on asset market volatility.

Table 2. Macroprudential Indicators in a Selection of Recent Studies

Studies by authors[1]	C-K	F-R	S-T-V	H	GH-P-B	B-G	B-P	E-L	E-R	F	H-P	K	K-L-R	R-S	DK-D
Year of publication	1996	1996	1996	1997	1997	1999	1999	1998	1998	1998	1998	1999	1998	1998	1998
Focus of study: B = banking crisis; C = currency crisis	B	C	C	B	B	C	C	C	B	C	B	B & C	C	C	B
Aggregated microprudential indicators															
Foreign exchange exposure		•		•					•	•		•			•
Sectoral credit concentration					•					•	•				
Nonperforming loans					•						•				
Aggregate risk-based capital ratio					•										
Central bank credits to financial institutions[2]				•							•	•			
Segmentation				•									•		
Ratio of deposits to M2 (or GDP)				•	•	•					•	•	•		
Stock exchange prices															
Aggregate average returns					•	•									
Macroeconomic indicators															
Lending booms (e.g., credit/GDP)	•		•	•		•	•	•		•	•	•		•	•
Asset price booms			•				•	•				•			•
Contagion effects			•				•	•							
External deficits		•					•	•			•			•	
Aggregated growth rate	•	•		•	•		•	•	•	•	•	•	•	•	•
Volatility of interest and exchange rates							•						•		
Terms of trade				•	•				•						
Level of domestic interest rates	•				•	•			•	•	•	•	•	•	•
Exchange rate misalignments		•		•	•	•						•		•	•
Government recourse to banking system												•			
Volatility in inflation				•	•										•

[1] Caprio and Klingebiel (C-K); Frankel and Rose (F-R); Sachs, Tornell, and Velasco (S-T-V); Honohan (H); González-Hermosillo, Pazarbaşioğlu, and Billings (GH-P-B); Baig and Goldfajn (B-G); Berg and Patillo (B-P); Esquivel and Larraín (E-L); Eichengreen and Rose (E-R); Fratzscher (F); Hardy and Pazarbaşioğlu (H-P); Kaminsky (K); Kaminsky, Lizondo, and Reinhart (K-L-R); Radelet and Sachs (R-S); and Demirgüç-Kunt and Detragiache (DK-D).

[2] As a proportion of their capital or liabilities.

studies investigate the vulnerability of financial institutions in the face of exogenous shocks. Financial intermediaries are generally highly leveraged, engage in maturity transformation, transact in markets with asymmetric information, and are subject to moral hazard through explicit or implicit deposit insurance. Sources of financial fragility explored in the studies include a falling growth rate, deterioration in the balance of payments, high inflation, volatile exchange rates, surges in stock market activity and prices, credit booms, weakening performance of export sectors, and deterioration in the terms of trade. In addition, these studies highlight nonquantifiable indicators of financial fragility, such as deficient banking supervision, inadequate instruments of monetary control, overly generous deposit insurance, inadequacies in the operation of the legal system, overexposure in international financial markets, lack of adequate accounting standards and practices, insufficient financial disclosure, and perverse incentive structures.

The Asian crisis has provoked a new wave of financial sector studies, which confirm that macroeconomic shocks to output, exports, prices and the terms of trade, asset price booms, and inappropriate monetary and exchange rate policies, all result in financial pressure and contribute to crises in financial systems that are inherently fragile.[44] In addition, this research points to the destabilizing effects of market overreaction, the feedback effects of crises that weaken corporate balance sheets, and the impact of unexpected shocks, such as the rapid change in the yen-dollar exchange rate and the swift emergence of new competition from Mexico (in the wake of the deep devaluation in 1994–95) and from China. These are important factors that must be evaluated in cases of economic instability. Except for the impact of third-party exchange rate changes on the domestic economy, however, these developments generally do not appear in advance of financial weakening and, therefore, do not offer additional early warning indicators of financial health.

The contagion of financial crises from one country to another has been the focus of several empirical studies.[45] The factors that appear to expose a country's financial system to contagion include close correlation in the past behavior of currency and equity markets, export and import ties (or competition in trade), cross-market banking links, low levels of foreign reserves, the extent of exchange rate overvalua-

tion, and the inherent weakness of the financial system. In addition, Kaminsky and Reinhart (1998) find evidence that sharing a common creditor with a crisis country creates a high risk of contagion.

Given that currency and financial crises often occur simultaneously, the factors underlying currency crises have the potential to contribute to an assessment of the health of financial institutions. Causation between exchange rates and financial variables, however, may go in either or both directions. This relationship has been the subject of several studies, including Dornbusch, Goldfajn, and Valdés (1995); Kaminsky and Reinhart (1999); Kaminsky (1999); and Kaminsky, Lizondo, and Reinhart (1998). Their results suggest that exchange rate crises provoke financial crises when the banking sector is vulnerable, that is, when the impact of a devaluation on the quality of bank assets is large enough to wipe out the banks' net worth. Therefore, simulations (stress tests) of the impact of a devaluation of various magnitudes on banks' capital adequacy can be useful as an additional indicator of financial robustness. Kaminsky and Reinhart (1999), however, point out that in about half of the crises in the 1980s and early 1990s that they examined, financial crises preceded currency crises.

Studies of Aggregated Microprudential Indicators

Much of the earlier literature on aggregated microprudential indicators follows the categorization of the CAMELS rating—see Altman (1968), Sinkey (1978), and Thomson (1991). This portfolio-based assessment method is broadly consistent with the list of MPIs identified in Section II. These variables are used in empirical research less frequently than macroeconomic indicators, due to the availability of higher frequency data for the latter. A classic study by Altman (1968) uses the so-called Z-score model, which is based on several financial ratios capturing asset quality, earnings performance, and liquidity, but this analysis is at the level of the individual firm.[46]

More recent literature—including Frankel and Rose (1996); Sachs, Tornell, and Velasco (1996); and Honohan (1997)—emphasizes the important role of foreign borrowing, particularly short-term liabilities denominated in foreign currency, to measure the degree of exposure to currency and inflation risks. Re-

---

[44]These studies include Berg and Patillo (1999), Bussière and Mulder (1999), Corsetti, Pesenti, and Roubini (1998), Furman and Stiglitz (1998), International Monetary Fund (1998), Kawai (1998), Kwack (1998), and Radelet and Sachs (1998).

[45]Baig and Goldfajn (1999), Fratzscher (1998), Glick and Rose (1998), and Sachs, Tornell, and Velasco (1996).

[46]The Z-score model uses the linear discriminant analysis method to identify healthy and unhealthy firms, and "Z" represents the composite score used to distinguish between these two groups of firms.

cent literature also focuses on the level of nonper-forming loans—such as González-Hermosillo, Pazarbaşioğlu and Billings (1997). González-Hermosillo (1999) shows empirical evidence that the CAMELS-type assessment is statistically significant only if nonperforming loans and capital adequacy are simultaneously considered.[47] This is consistent with theoretical explanations for the eruption of the Asian financial crisis, which posit financial institutions' weaknesses as a major cause of the crisis.

Other indicators to capture financial vulnerability include a measure of segmentation (often proxied by an interbank interest rate differential), the deposits-to-M2 ratio, and aggregate stock indices. In surveying literature on these indicators, Demirgüç-Kunt and Detragiache (1999) point to criticisms on the use of CAMELS-based criteria to measure bank strength. A comprehensive study by Kaminsky, Lizondo, and Reinhart (1998) concludes that these indicators are less able to explain currency crises than is exchange rate misalignment.

Many of these studies use logit/probit models to capture banking fragility or to differentiate healthy banks from unhealthy banks. But their ability to detect future events in the out-of-sample forecasting context is limited. Lane, Looney, and Wansley (1986) and Whalen (1991) use the Cox proportional hazards model, which is capable of providing information on the expected time of failure, but the overall conclusion on the poor performance of the CAMELS-type model remains unchanged. Consequently, González-Hermosillo (1999) combines both micro- and macro-factors in explaining banking fragility, and concludes that the introduction of macroeconomic variables sig-nificantly improves the explanatory power of models based on microprudential indicators only.

Indicators of capital adequacy provide important information about financial fragility. Minimum standards for risk-weighted capital adequacy have been agreed to by the Basel Committee on Banking Supervision, but there remain reservations about these standards, which are currently under review.[48] The literature points to some of these limitations. For example, the Basel Committee on Banking Supervision (BIS (1999b)) shows that the improvement in the ratio for Group of Ten (G–10) countries from 9.3 in 1988 to 11.2 percent in 1996 did not reflect a significant improvement in the overall health of the system.[49] Proposals currently under discussion at the Basel Committee would supplement capital adequacy measures with supervisory reviews that could require higher levels of capitalization and use different measures of risk exposure, such as the increasingly popular Value-at-Risk (VaR) models.[50]

---

[47]This study includes a recent survey of empirical studies on banking failures.

[48]The Basel Committee's recent recommendations on capital adequacy (still in the form of a discussion draft) can be found in BIS (1999a).

[49]BIS (1999b) also points out that the way in which undercapitalized banks meet the minimum capital requirement depends on individual cases. Ediz, Michael, and Perraudin (1998) show that banks in the United Kingdom tend to raise their Tier 2 capital first, followed by their Tier 1 capital.

[50]Value-at-Risk is an estimate of the maximum loss on a portfolio with a given (small) probability over a preset horizon. The VaR methodology uses a standard statistical technique usually based on the historical volatility and correlation of portfolio returns to measure market risk (not credit risk)—see Hendricks (1996), and Dimson and Marsh (1997). While the incorporation of VaR models into capital adequacy regulation could permit a more accurate estimation of risk, it should be noted that there are drawbacks to VaR models. In particular, these models are unable to account for shocks that depart considerably from past experience (e.g., a large devaluation).

IV   Work Programs of Other Institutions

In response to the recent crises, many institutions have initiated or intensified work on developing macroprudential indicators and macroprudential analysis capabilities. A selection of these efforts is summarized in this section. The statistical frameworks that are in place in some of the institutions are discussed in Appendix I.

International and Multilateral Institutions

European Central Bank

Upon the request of the European Central Bank (ECB) Banking Supervision Committee (BSC), the ECB's Working Group on Financial Fragility has carried out preliminary work on MPIs. This working group separated potential indicators into three categories: (1) systemic indicators of the health of the banking system, (2) macroeconomic factors that influence the banking system, and (3) contagion factors. With regard to the first category, it proposed the monitoring of the following variables: lending behavior, competitive conditions, liquidity situation, exposure concentrations, asset quality, profitability, capital buffers, and market assessments. The macroeconomic indicators suggested as factors that influence the banking system were income development, leverage (financial fragility), debt burden, asset prices, monetary conditions, and the external position.[51]

The BSC has recently established the Working Group on Macroprudential Analysis. The mandate of the working group is to develop a framework for macroprudential analysis following the approaches of several Scandinavian countries (explained below).

Based on this framework, the group is to draft a report on European Union (EU)-wide MPIs that would serve as a basis for BSC discussion of the soundness and characteristics of the EU banking systems. The framework would draw on economic statistics as well as supervisory insights. Currently there are no plans to make the results of the exercise public. The BSC also operates the Cooperative Forum on Early Warning Systems, with voluntary participation by interested EU member states. Even though these projects are facilitated by the relatively high degree of harmonization of standards within the EU, comparability of indicators among member states is complicated by, among other factors, remaining differences in accounting and provisioning norms.

World Bank

The World Bank has been conducting Financial Sector Assessments (FSAs) for a number of countries where it is involved in financial sector work and where financial sector issues are considered particularly relevant to the World Bank's lending decisions. These assessments are focused on both stability and developmental aspects of the financial sector and contain an analysis of a range of MPIs, both macroeconomic indicators as well as banking indicators. The latter are drawn primarily from public data (published accounts). In order to avoid overlap and duplication of work in this area, the IMF and the World Bank have recently established a joint framework for comprehensive assessments of financial sectors, the FSAP.[52]

In addition to the more qualitative FSAs, the Country Credit Risk Department of the World Bank uses various risk-rating models in order to determine the likelihood of default of its borrowers. These models include a checklist model that is more complex but otherwise very similar to the ones used by rating agencies and investment banks. The main areas covered by this model are (1) structural and macroeconomic indicators of economic performance

---

[51]These indicators are to be analyzed in their relation to the following intermediate risk targets: aggregate credit risk, interest rate risk, equity price risk, real estate risk, foreign exchange risk, and liquidity risk. The ultimate target variable is the aggregate solvency of the banking system. The analysis under the first category would draw on confidential supervisory data, whereas the analysis under the second would be based largely on public information as well as on available macroeconomic forecasts.

[52]See Section V for details.

and external vulnerability, (2) external debt and its sustainability, (3) political risk and policy performance, and (4) World Bank exposure and history of debt service to the Bank.

The Country Credit Risk Department is also the secretariat of the Short-Term Risk Monitoring Group of the World Bank. This group is responsible for assessing and monitoring countries that are vulnerable to political, economic, or financial crises in the near term. The group reports to the senior management of the World Bank on both vulnerable countries and trends in the global economy and financial markets on a monthly basis. A country's vulnerability to domestic or exogenous shocks is assessed using macroeconomic and policy performance indicators (including indices developed by some of the World Bank's regional departments), financial market indicators, and qualitative assessments provided by operational and central units, including financial sector specialists. As the secretariat of the group, the Country Credit Risk Department is also responsible for assisting operational units in preparing contingency plans for countries that are considered highly vulnerable. These contingency plans are intended to ensure a broad understanding of the situation in the country concerned and to facilitate a discussion by senior management of the World Bank's response.

G–7 and G–10 Initiatives

The G–7 endorsed, in February 1999, a proposal by Hans Tietmeyer, former president of the Bundesbank, to establish the Financial Stability Forum (FSF). The forum comprises representatives from the G–7 countries plus Australia, Hong Kong SAR, the Netherlands, Singapore, the IMF, the World Bank, the Bank for International Settlements (BIS), the OECD, the Basel Committee on Banking Supervision, the International Organization of Securities Commissions (IOSCO), the International Association of Insurance Supervisors (IAIS), the Committee on Payment and Settlement Systems (CPSS), and the Committee on the Global Financial System (CGFS). Part of the mandate of the FSF is to strengthen the monitoring and assessment of systemic vulnerabilities. The FSF has established three working groups dealing with highly leveraged institutions, capital flows, and offshore financial centers, respectively. In addition, a task force on implementation of standards and study groups on deposit insurance and insurance issues have been set up. A study paper on Internet and electronic trading in financial markets has also been commissioned. It appears that the FSF will primarily focus on specific areas of systemic vulnerability of the financial system and not on the continuous monitoring of large sets of indicators.

The CGFS has a mandate from the governors of the central banks of the G–10 member countries. It acts as a central bank forum for the monitoring and examination of broad issues relating to financial markets and systems with a view to elaborating appropriate policy recommendations to support the central banks in the fulfillment of their responsibilities for monetary and financial stability. The tasks performed by the CGFS fall into three categories: systematic short-term monitoring of global financial system conditions, so as to identify potential sources of stress; in-depth, longer-term analysis of the functioning of financial markets; and the articulation of policy recommendations aimed at improving market functioning and promoting stability. The mandate recognizes that the causes of financial instability can arise from both the behavior of markets and the complex interrelationships that exist between institutions, markets, infrastructures, and macroeconomic policy.

Non-G–10 central banks now routinely attend meetings of the CGFS and participate in its working groups. In recent public reports, the committee has focused on the nature and use of information available for banks' country risk assessments; it has identified general principles and more specific policy recommendations for the promotion of liquid government securities markets; and it has examined the events surrounding the financial turbulence in many international markets in autumn 1998.[53] One of its working groups has formulated a set of public disclosure guidelines to provide a meaningful basis for comparing levels and types of risk across institutions and across countries. This work, in turn, has been incorporated in a multidisciplinary effort comprising representatives from the banking, securities, and insurance regulators. A pilot effort involving private sector firms is to be conducted.

The G–10 Working Party on Financial Stability in Emerging Market Economies published a report on financial stability in emerging markets in April 1997. This report identifies both macroeconomic sources of vulnerability (instability, inflation, liberalization, and failures in the design of macroeconomic policy instruments), as well as sector-specific sources of vulnerability (corporate governance and management, market infrastructure and discipline, and supervision and regulation). The report also contains a list of indicators of robust financial systems. These indicators are categorized under the following six groupings: (1) legal and judicial framework; (2) accounting, disclosure, and transparency; (3) stakeholder oversight and institutional governance; (4) market structure; (5) supervisory and regulatory

---

[53]BIS, Committee on the Global Financial System (1999).

authority; and (6) design of a safety net. Under these categories, the report lists areas of importance, but not specific indicators. The areas mentioned are broadly equivalent to those identified by other institutions, including the IMF.

National Central Banks and Supervisory Agencies

Until recently, relatively few countries paid in-depth attention to macroprudential analysis at the national level, although national central banks and supervisory agencies in many countries have long monitored and reported on issues relating to financial system stability. While much of this work has a macroprudential aspect, it is not necessarily carried out with a formal framework for using MPIs to assess financial system soundness.[54] The complex nature of the analysis and the need for high-quality data on individual banks, collected and stored in a manner conducive to aggregation and analysis, has meant that much of the existing MPI-related work has been carried out relatively recently and mainly, but not exclusively, in the industrial countries. Within this group, the most developed approaches tend to be those by countries that have had a major financial sector crisis in recent years. Work is, however, currently under way in a number of countries to develop macroprudential data collection and analysis frameworks.

Following is a selective country-by-country summary of work that has been carried out, both with a specific focus on identifying MPIs, and with other focuses that may, nevertheless, provide a guide to possible MPIs. Table 3 gives a comparative listing of indicators used in a few selected countries. The listing is certainly not comprehensive—neither with respect to the countries nor the indicators being used. Rather, our intent is to provide a sketch of the different types of approaches and key indicators.

As a general observation, to the extent that specific MPIs are identified for a given country, they tend to be aggregated microprudential indicators rather than macroeconomic indicators. This may reflect the fact that while it is generally possible to identify the ex post macroeconomic variables that have contributed to systemic problems, it is difficult,

ex ante, to predict the macroeconomic developments that may trigger problems, or their precise timing. Nonetheless, it is clear that macroeconomic indicators play a central role in almost all macroprudential analysis frameworks. As a further observation, while the indicators monitored in different countries are broadly similar, where differences do arise they often reflect country-specific characteristics of past financial sector problems.

China

As with many other countries, the Chinese authorities are in the early stages of building a framework for macroprudential analysis. A range of indicators to be collected and monitored has been identified. Macroeconomic variables include GDP, inflation, monetary aggregates, the current account balance, external debt, international reserves, and the exchange rate. Aggregated microprudential indicators, building on the off-site supervision of commercial banks, include indicators of general performance (trends in total assets, loans, and deposits); safety indicators (capital adequacy, asset quality, and credit concentration); liquidity indicators (liquidity of assets, excess reserves, and liquidity of domestic and foreign currency liabilities); earnings indicators (return on equity and assets); and overall control indicators (loan to deposit ratios, proportion of interbank financing, and proportion of offshore financing).

The People's Bank of China is currently working to further develop a framework for collecting and analyzing MPIs. The ongoing transition to a market economy means that parts of the financial infrastructure—such as accounting and auditing practices—are still being developed. In addition, prudential data quality may vary across different regions of the country. Improvements are under way in the area of regulation and supervision of financial institutions, including upgrading loan classification standards, and strengthening the supervisory capabilities of the central bank, which will enhance the quality of macroprudential analyses.

Finland

The Bank of Finland is one of the few central banks to have a framework for forecasting banking sector developments. In addition, the Bank of Finland is actively participating in the work being undertaken by the ECB in developing a system of MPIs. The banking forecast framework was developed in the wake of Finland's banking sector crisis in the early 1990s, with a view to assisting in its resolution by analyzing likely developments in the banking sector. The framework produces a forecast of trends in banking system profitability over about a

---

[54]As an example, the Reserve Bank of India prepares an annual report on banking trends in India in terms of a statutory requirement under the Banking Regulation Act of 1949. The report covers developments in banking policy, cooperative banking, banks and nonbanking institutions, and provides some information on MPIs, including financial ratios, off-balance sheet exposures, nonperforming loans, and profitability. The Reserve Bank of India, however, does not report the use of these MPIs in any formal framework covering systemic soundness.

Table 3. Comparative Listing of Indicators Used by Selected Country Authorities

| | | | United States | |
| | | | Federal Reserve | Federal Deposit Insurance Corporation |
	Bank of Finland[1]	Norges Bank[2]	Sveriges Riksbank	Financial Institutions Monitoring System	Growth Management System
Banking sector variables	Assessments of bank profitability Assessments of loan losses and other write-offs	Capital/assets ratios Profitability trends Return on assets Gross interest margins Spread between short- and long-term interest rates Operating costs trends Deposits/loans ratios Deposit, loan growth rates Trends in riskiness of corporate debt Sectoral debt and debt-servicing ratios Forecast past-due loans Trends in bank financing from other sources	Profitability trends Return on assets Gross interest margins Spread between short- and long-term interest rates Operating costs trends Banks' share prices Bankruptcy trends Trends in past due loans by sector Sectoral debt and debt-servicing ratios Counterparties' risk exposure	Tangible capital/assets ratio Loans past due, 30–89 days Loans past due, 90 days or more Nonaccrual loans Foreclosed real estate Net income/assets ratio Reserves Investment securities/assets ratio UBSS asset growth percentile score[3] UBSS composite percentile score[3] Prior management rating Prior composite CAMEL rating	Equity/assets ratio Asset growth Loan growth Volatile liabilities/assets Loans/assets ratio Portfolio concentration[4] Growth in portfolio concentration[4] Equity/assets growth Loans/assets growth[4] Volatile liabilities/assets growth[4,5]
Macroeconomic variables	Market interest and exchange rates Asset prices Output and income Savings and investment Monetary aggregates Balance of payments	Impact of interest rate changes Growth rate of lending Asset prices GDP growth Corporate debt levels	Level of real interest rates Growth rate of lending Trends in inflation and expectations Trends in intermediation and competition		

[1]Variables used to forecast bank profitability.

[2]Includes separate analysis of savings banks and securities markets.

[3]The output from the Uniform Bank Surveillance System (UBSS) is inputted to the FIMS. The UBSS ranks institutions' financial ratios relative to those of their peer groups, so as to identify which institutions are performing relatively poorly.

[4]These variables have been tested to see if they improve model performance.

[5]Volatile liabilities are defined as the sum of: time deposits of $100,000 or more; deposits in foreign offices; federal funds purchase and repurchase agreements; demand notes issued to the U.S. Treasury; and other liabilities for borrowed money.

two-year time span. While the framework can highlight areas of vulnerability in the banking system through the impact on profits, it is not focused on identifying specific vulnerabilities. Potential vulnerabilities, however, are taken into consideration in the sensitivity analyses.

The framework is formally linked to the Bank of Finland's macro forecasting model of the Finnish economy. As such, it incorporates a number of macroeconomic variables (for example, GDP growth and interest rates) as inputs to forecast the components of gross income, while the outputs of the framework (bank profitability, and bank lending and deposit interest rates) are inputs to the model. There is thus a feedback relationship between the framework and the macro model, requiring iterations between the two forecast procedures. Data inputs to the framework are used to develop forecasts of the various components of the banking system's gross income and expenses, which are then aggregated to produce an estimated trend in banking sector profitability over the forecast time frame.

Norway

Norges Bank has produced reports on the situation and outlook for the financial sector since 1995.[55] The work includes both analyses of developments in financial institutions, primarily in the banking sector, and the relationship between macroeconomic and financial sector developments. Analyses of the financial position of households and enterprises are important elements of this framework. The reports are for the internal use of the financial sector authorities and are not published. Norges Bank has published excerpts, however, in the second and fourth editions of each year's quarterly *Economic Bulletin* since 1997. In keeping with the summary approach being taken, the published reports are relatively qualitative, with overall assessments of financial health rather than a focus on critical values of specific indicators.

The approach taken is to generate an initial assessment of the trends in macroeconomic variables that are of relevance to the financial sector and, in particular, to the earnings of financial institutions. These variables include economic growth, interest rates, credit growth, and sectoral debt levels. Following this analysis, a range of individual indicators of the financial health of the banking system are incorporated in the assessment (e.g., capital adequacy ratios, credit growth rates, trends in overdue loans, interest rate trends, and trends in operating costs). Specific attention is paid to the banks' exposures to the real estate market. Given that past experience has shown

that enterprise sector loans have been a major source of bank losses, attention is also paid to the exposure of banks to the enterprise sector, as well as to the ability of firms in that sector to cope with an unexpected deterioration in their financial condition and to stay current with their debt servicing. A similar sectoral analysis is conducted of the financial condition of the household sector. The analysis also covers recent trends in aggregate bank profits, including the components of earnings and expenses, and other balance sheet items. The objective is to identify trends, as well as to explain them. Finally, attention is paid to the risks arising from financial institutions' exposure to the securities markets.

Sweden

The Swedish approach to assessing banking system health is similar to the one followed in Norway. It is somewhat more formalized but does not follow a model approach as in the case of Finland. The assessments are carried out by the Sveriges Riksbank in the context of its responsibility to promote a safe and efficient payment system, as set out in the Riksbank Act. Given the integration of the payment system with the financial system as a whole, the Riksbank's surveillance of payment system developments encompasses systemic issues relating to banking system stability. The Riksbank's surveillance is directed toward systems and markets and, therefore, complements the supervision of the banking system by the Swedish Financial Supervision Authority, which is primarily aimed at individual institutions.

Since 1997, the Riksbank has been publishing reviews of the banking system on a semiannual basis.[56] The approach clearly starts with the payment system. It focuses on aggregated risks, rather than bank-specific issues. A major objective of the reports is to raise the financial sector's awareness of vulnerability issues. The method is to assess risks to aggregate banking sector profits based on information from the markets, on a sector-by-sector basis. The assessments are carried out by looking at three categories of risk that affect banks' abilities to generate profits: (1) strategic risks, or factors affecting profit generation over the longer term; (2) credit risks, or risks to profits over the medium term; and (3) counterparty and settlement risks, or risks that affect profits over short and very short terms.

A list of the variables that are examined in the Swedish approach is presented in Table 3. The list is

---

[55]Norges Bank (1998).

[56]The first three reports in this series—called *Financial Market Reports*—focused on an in-depth presentation of several key aspects of the analysis. Subsequent reports—renamed *Financial Stability Reports*—have provided updates of the analysis. See Sveriges Riksbank (1999).

indicative, partly because the approach incorporates a large number of variables, and partly because some aspects of the analysis are qualitative—for instance, the speed of deregulation, the degree of competition in the banking sector, and assessments of key risk management features—and, therefore, do not lend themselves to inclusion in a listing of quantitative indicators. The macroeconomic variables that are reviewed include the growth rate of aggregate lending, the rate of change in inflation, changes in inflation expectations, and the level of real interest rates. Several banking sector variables are also reviewed, including profits, the degree of disintermediation, bankruptcies, loan performance by sector, and debt-servicing capabilities by sector.

United Kingdom

Under a 1997 Memorandum of Understanding between the United Kingdom Treasury, the Bank of England, and the Financial Services Authority, the Bank of England is responsible for the stability of the financial system as a whole.[57] A Standing Committee of the Treasury, the Bank of England, and the Financial Services Authority meets monthly to discuss developments relevant to financial stability. One of the tasks that the Bank of England undertakes to discharge its responsibility is the surveillance of financial stability conditions, including the assessment of actual or potential shocks, and of the system's capacity to absorb shocks. The Financial Stability Area of the Bank of England undertakes a monthly assessment of financial stability and produces a variety of more narrowly focused notes. A more thorough review of the financial stability conjuncture and outlook is undertaken every six months and a version is published in the Bank of England's *Financial Stability Review*.[58] The review also includes articles relating to the assessment of risks to financial stability. While the monthly assessments are used to inform some other public documents, the assessments themselves are not published.

Rather than use complex models, the Bank of England's approach is to review a range of information from the United Kingdom, industrial economies, and emerging market economies and try to identify key developments, vulnerabilities, and risks that could affect financial stability. While the Bank of England is exploring the use of aggregated microprudential data covering groups of institutions in this work, and financial market data naturally play a key role, macroeconomic indicators are also re-

garded as important for financial-stability analysis (e.g., saving-investment balances and external balance sheets).

There are some problems with compiling aggregated microprudential data, as the existing data reporting systems were designed to support the supervision of individual institutions rather than surveillance of the system as a whole. Work is being undertaken by the Bank of England, together with the Financial Services Authority, to address this issue so that, for example, better analysis of peer groups of banks can be carried out. In addition to its work in this area, the Bank of England is seeking to develop its use of MPIs. This work includes identifying MPIs that might be useful in general, rather than specifically for the United Kingdom, and reviewing general issues relating to macroprudential surveillance.[59]

United States

The three institutions that have responsibility for different aspects of banking supervision—the Federal Deposit Insurance Corporation (FDIC), the Federal Reserve, and the Office of the Comptroller of the Currency (OCC)—have, over time, developed similar models and indicators aimed at assessing the overall health of individual banks based on summary data submitted by the banks as part of their off-site supervision exercises. Aggregating the information for individual banks can provide assessments of the health of significant components of the financial system. Work has also been carried out, for example, by the Federal Reserve, to identify macroeconomic variables that could be incorporated in predictive frameworks. While individual variables have been found to be significant within sample, none have significantly improved out-of-sample predictive power.

In general, the variables used in the assessments of the future health of individual banks by the supervisory institutions in the United States are proxies for the various factors taken into account when performing a full ex post CAMELS rating. These variables for an individual bank may be useful as MPIs when one or more banks individually are sufficiently large to have systemic implications. At an aggregated level for the banking system, the variables that have been found to be significant in assessing the current health of a bank may be used as MPIs. As an example, the variables used by the Federal Reserve in its Financial Institutions Monitoring System (FIMS) exercise to assess the current health of a bank are included in Table 3 (see page 21).[60]

---

[57]Responsibility for the authorization and supervision of individual financial institutions and providers of financial infrastructure rests with the Financial Services Authority.

[58]Bank of England (1999).

[59]Davis (1999).

[60]For a description of the FIMS, see Cole, Cornyn, and Gunther (1995).

As an extension of the assessments of current health of individual banks, the U.S. supervisory agencies have also worked on models for assessing the current riskiness of banks that can generate probabilities of future failure. To the extent that these models perform successfully, they can be used to focus scarce on-site supervision resources on those banks judged to be at the highest risk, and to take early steps to reduce those risks. Again, the variables used could be useful as MPIs. As an example of the MPIs that might be derived from this approach, the variables used by the FDIC in its Growth Management System (GMS) to assess probabilities of future bank failures are also provided in Table 3.[61] Some of the variables that are being examined for possible future inclusion in the FDIC model are included in this table as well.

The computerized statistical system that supports the work of the three agencies permits joint collection of income, operating activity, and balance sheet data for individual banks, which are roughly disaggregated into national and worldwide components. The system generates statistics for a variety of purposes by each agency, such as supporting the supervision of individual institutions, econometric research, and aggregation into macroeconomic statistics. The data are regularly used for multivariate cross-section or time-series analyses of income or balance sheet items. Also, the data are aggregated by the Federal Reserve into the sectoral balance sheets used in the flow of funds and the national accounts. Thus, it is a fully integrated system that permits supervisory, statistical, and econometric analysis of microdata, sectoral structural data, and macroeconomic data.

Indicators Used by Investors and Rating Agencies

Private investors such as banks, securities firms, and investment funds use various indicators to evaluate the vulnerability of financial systems. The primary purpose is to determine the creditworthiness of borrowers and issuers that have significant exposure to a particular financial system.[62] Such analysis is generally based on three kinds of indicators:

- *Indicators published by official sources*—the government and central bank, as well as international financial institutions, such as the IMF, the World Bank, and the BIS.

- *In-house analyses of vulnerability of financial systems.* This type of analysis, which some financial institutions conduct, is often based on well-established indicators such as CAMELS ratings, rather than on comprehensive macroprudential models. Main sources for the indicators are IMF or World Bank publications. Indicators of the vulnerability of individual borrowers and issuers—an area where financial institutions do have a comparative advantage through their business relationship—are considered proprietary information and are usually not publicly available.

- *Creditworthiness ratings by credit rating agencies.* Most investors still regard ratings as the best available indicators of vulnerability, even though the limitations of ratings are well recognized.

For most investors, credit rating agencies are the primary source of information on the creditworthiness of individual financial institutions (issuer and debt ratings), and on the creditworthiness of the government (sovereign risk ratings). Both ratings taken together can serve as an indicator of market perceptions of the vulnerability of a country's financial system.

For *sovereign ratings*, the most commonly used indicators are recent economic performance, the quality of economic and financial management, the depth and sophistication of markets, the stability of economic policy, the stability and effectiveness of the political system, and long-term trends and expected future performance. Particular emphasis is often given to the quality of economic management, the stability of policy, and the depth and sophistication of local markets. Some agencies use methodologies geared more toward macroeconomic indicators such as income and economic structure, economic growth prospects, fiscal flexibility, public debt burden, price stability, balance of payments flexibility, and external debt and liquidity, as well as political risk. Recent studies have found that creditworthiness ratings appear to be determined primarily by economic events, rather than political variables. Moreover, following the Asian crisis, rating agencies are placing greater emphasis on factors such as external debt and liquidity, banking soundness, and corporate leverage.[63]

For *bank ratings*, indicators include quantitative factors such as asset quality, capital adequacy, profitability and liquidity, as well as qualitative factors such as environment, business franchise values,

---

[61]For a description of the GMS, see Federal Deposit Insurance Corporation (1997), Vol. I, pp. 496–507. The OCC has been using a variety of computer applications to monitor financial institutions' risks; see FDIC (1997), Vol. I, p. 512.

[62]The indicators used by private investors need to be differentiated from the so-called market-based indicators, such as stock market and bond indices.

---

[63]See Haque, Mark, and Mathieson (1998), and International Monetary Fund (1999c).

management quality, hidden strengths and reserves, and hidden weaknesses and overvalued assets.[64] In addition to publishing issuer ratings, rating agencies also compile ratings of particular debt issues. In the case of bank debt issues, their usefulness as an MPI may be limited by the fact that these ratings usually incorporate an evaluation of the likelihood of government support.[65] Therefore, in addition to those traditional ratings, some agencies have developed ratings that are designed to indicate financial strength on a stand-alone basis.[66] Such ratings reflect the probability that outside assistance will be needed, but not the probability that it will be provided. In practice, *financial strength ratings* primarily look at bank-specific elements such as financial fundamentals, franchise value, and business and asset diversification, but also take into account the bank's operating environment, including the strength and prospective performance of the economy, as well as the structure and relative fragility of the financial system, and the quality of banking regulation and supervision.

---

[64]Standard and Poor's (1999), Fitch IBCA (1998), and Thomson Financial Bankwatch (1999).

[65]Government support is often assumed in the presence of government guarantees, government or quasi-government ownership or control, high concentration in the banking system, or by precedent.

[66]Moody's Investors Service (1999). See also the discussion of market-based indicators in Section II.

V   IMF Initiatives

IMF surveillance of member countries' economies under Article IV of its charter has always included, to some degree, the surveillance of financial systems, primarily with the aim of ensuring the effective functioning of monetary and exchange policy. Article IV staff reports have, on occasion, contained special annexes dealing with financial sector developments, but in-depth surveillance by the IMF of financial systems was generally limited, with the focus being primarily on the IMF's provision of technical assistance in specific areas identified by member countries or previous IMF missions.

Reports and Publications

Within the framework of multilateral surveillance, the IMF Research Department has published the *International Capital Markets* report annually since 1980. This report summarizes and analyzes developments in international financial markets, including financial market indicators that may signal vulnerabilities in the global financial system. The report draws, in part, on a series of informal discussions with commercial and investment banks, securities firms, stock and futures exchanges, regulatory and monetary authorities, and the staffs of international organizations such as the BIS, the European Commission, the International Swaps and Derivatives Association, and the OECD.

Similarly, the IMF Research Department regularly analyzes developments of market-based indicators, including international bond issuance, international loans and loan facilities, stock market and bond indices (including spreads), and ratings by international rating agencies. These data, which reflect market sentiment toward a country's economy, and particularly its financial system, may serve as useful indicators of financial system vulnerability.[67]

In 1996 the IMF published *Bank Soundness and Macroeconomic Policy*, its first major analysis of the interaction between these two topics.[68] The analysis highlights the issues posed by current or potential banking system unsoundness in four policy areas: the design and implementation of stabilization programs, the use of monetary instruments, the implications for fiscal policy, and the management of international capital flows. It outlines key structural policy issues relevant to maintaining a sound banking system and examines how the IMF might better incorporate banking sector considerations into its surveillance, program design, and technical assistance work. The book also contains a survey of indicators for predicting bank unsoundness, primarily those based on individual bank supervisory information, as used by supervisory authorities and central banks.

In January 1998, the IMF published a survey entitled *Toward a Framework for Financial Stability*.[69] The survey sets out, among other things, guidelines on the quality of information indicating financial system vulnerabilities to be used for supervisory reporting and public disclosure. The guidelines are based on internationally accepted standards, where they exist, and refer to both qualitative and quantitative information. Issues covered are, for example, accounting and valuation rules, loan portfolio review and classification, treatment of collateral, and loan loss provisioning. Adherence to internationally accepted minimum standards in these areas is considered an essential precondition for the use of macroprudential data as useful indicators of vulnerability.

Surveillance Procedures and Operations

Financial System Surveillance

In 1998, the Monetary and Exchange Affairs Department (MAE) issued an internal guidance note designed to facilitate discussions on financial system issues between the IMF staff and the national authorities in the context of Article IV surveillance. It suggests specific areas for discussion including the following topics:

---

[67]The Research Department also runs an ongoing project to analyze, on an experimental basis, the results of early warning system models.

[68]Lindgren, Garcia, and Saal (1996).
[69]Folkerts-Landau and Lindgren (1998).

- *Sectoral indicators of the health of the banking and financial system.* Indicators of the health of the financial system identified as high priority include the foreign exchange exposure of financial institutions, sectoral credit concentration, exposure to large holdings of securities, the aggregate ratio of nonperforming loans to total loans, the aggregate risk-based capital ratio, and central bank credits to banks and other financial institutions as a proportion of their capital or their liabilities.

- *Macroeconomic factors that impact the financial system.* This is a set of indicators concerning macroeconomic developments that could affect the financial system, with the following indicators considered as high priority: lending booms, asset price booms, high corporate leverage ratios, contagion effects, rises in the ratio of the external account deficit to GDP, low or declining aggregate growth rates, and volatility in exchange and interest rates.

- *Elements for the assessment of the institutional and regulatory frameworks.* The focus here is on assessing the adequacy of a broad range of public policies and frameworks affecting the financial system and the incentive structure, and the likelihood of the authorities to adhere and enforce best principles and practices. In this context, Article IV missions are asked to look at the structure of the financial system, public disclosure and the accounting and legal frameworks, incentive structures and safety nets, prudential regulations and supervision, and liberalization and deregulation processes.[70]

- *Main effects of financial system distress.* The guidance note highlights the main macroeconomic effects of financial system problems in terms of direct monetary effects, direct fiscal effects, quasi-fiscal effects, and other macroeconomic impacts. The guidance note also recommends that these effects be assessed, incorporated in macroeconomic estimates and projections, and discussed with the authorities. In case contingent liabilities are identified, it is suggested that IMF staff prepare alternative scenarios of possible additional monetary and fiscal effects.

Complementing the guidance note, MAE transmitted to area and functional departments, a set of related tables and questionnaires. These tables and questionnaires focus on the structure and performance of the financial sector and the legal and regulatory framework for banking supervision. In addition, there is a summary table that may be included in Article IV reports. The tables and questionnaires are designed to be either sent to the country in advance, and then discussed during the mission, or completed during the Article IV mission itself. MAE then collects the information obtained from the tables and questionnaires and enters it into a databank for future reference (the databank now contains about 20 countries). Both the guidance note and the accompanying tables and questionnaires are being used by all missions involved in monitoring financial sectors under IMF surveillance.

Financial Sector Assessment Program and Financial System Stability Assessments

Based on the guidance note and building on work already conducted in various countries in the context of Article IV surveillance and the use of IMF resources missions, MAE has recently established an enhanced monitoring mechanism for financial systems through in-depth FSSAs. FSSAs are conducted within the framework of the joint World Bank-IMF FSAP.[71] These assessments are designed to provide an instrument to highlight strengths, risks, and vulnerabilities in the financial sector, as well as the linkages between financial system developments and macroeconomic outcomes in the context of IMF surveillance, program design, and related technical assistance. They also involve an assessment of observance of standards, core principles, and good practices in the financial sector, as needed.

The key structural and institutional components that contribute to financial system stability are grouped into four categories: official oversight and regulations, systemic liquidity developments and policy, arrangements for crisis management and restructuring, and major risk exposures, including systemic risks in the payment, clearing, and settlement systems. These components are to be reviewed and assessed in a comprehensive manner, taking into account the macroeconomic environment and the broader structural reforms that are under way. This process is aimed at:

- identifying potential vulnerabilities of financial institutions and markets to macroeconomic shocks;
- evaluating the macroeconomic consequences of financial system vulnerabilities and reform; and

---

[70]These processes increase opportunities for financial institutions and markets to further develop, but may also expose financial institutions to new and more significant risks, while at the same time putting pressure on margins through increased competition.

[71]For background on the FSAP and FSSAs, see footnote 1.

• developing and sequencing key structural reforms and restructuring actions to promote financial system stability.

The appropriate sequencing of these reform components is to take into account the technical and operational linkages among them and their macroeconomic impact.

Both recent IMF initiatives—the guidance note and the FSSAs—have at their core an analysis of MPIs. Therefore, the analysis of MPIs forms an integral part of the IMF's financial system surveillance. The set of indicators that the IMF has identified so far, through its work on financial systems over many years, primarily encompasses the indicators discussed in Section II. The IMF Executive Board has recently endorsed additional research and analysis within the IMF to identify additional indicators that can be useful either generally or in the context of particular country circumstances. This work also aims at selecting a more limited set of MPIs that could be monitored by the IMF on an ongoing basis as part of its surveillance activities. It is expected that the experience with FSSAs will contribute to further progress in the analysis of MPIs.

VI   Measurement Issues

This section reviews statistical issues pertaining to the two major types of statistical information used in macroprudential analysis: macroeconomic indicators pertaining to the financial sector (financial macrostatistics) and aggregated microprudential data. Financial macrostatistics—such as monetary statistics, financial accounts of the System of National Accounts (SNA), and sectoral balance sheets—are frameworks for organizing data into comprehensive overviews of the condition and transactions of the financial sector and its key components, and thus can provide indicators of the activity and operation of the financial system. Aggregated microprudential data are summations of (mostly) supervisory information on the condition of individual banks that may provide indications of the overall condition of the financial sector.

We examine key issues affecting the statistical accuracy, usefulness, and international comparability of MPIs, and consider how the IMF could integrate work on MPIs into its statistical programs and support national authorities in the compilation of timely and reliable statistics needed to assess the condition of the financial system. Appendix I reviews the statistical frameworks for compilation of macroprudential data that are in place at the IMF, other international organizations, and selected central banks and supervisory agencies, and reviews the suitability of these frameworks for compilation of macroprudential data.[72]

The importance of reliable statistics in the assessment of the condition of the financial sector is well established. Unfortunately, in a significant number of problem cases, available statistics have not been of sufficient timeliness and/or quality to provide early and clear warning of emerging difficulties. In this connection, the importance and quality of monetary, balance of payments, and financial system data, as well as the need for comprehensiveness in the collection, methodological soundness of the compila-

tion, accuracy of compilation, and timely and informative public disclosure have often been emphasized. Moreover, comparability of MPIs across countries contributes strongly to their usefulness, a point emphasized at the September 1999 consultative meeting by private sector users of MPIs. Such comparability can be achieved through adherence of MPIs to internationally agreed supervisory, accounting, and statistical standards that provide clear rules for both the compilation and interpretation of MPIs.

Financial macrostatistics and aggregated microprudential data, which are both used in macroprudential analysis, interrelate in numerous ways because both are derived from individual banks' balance sheets and other detailed financial information. The two types of data could be brought into closer correspondence by applying standard statistical concepts (such as definitions of residency, sectors, and financial instruments) when compiling aggregate microprudential data, and by enhancing financial macrostatistics with additional detail needed for macroprudential analysis (such as information on nonperforming loans).

Statistical Frameworks for MPIs

Financial Macrostatistics

Nearly all countries compile financial sector macroeconomic statistics, primarily in the form of monetary statistics. However, monetary statistics generally do not provide the specific types of data used for macroprudential analysis or may lack needed detail. Other financial statistics frameworks, such as flow of funds accounts or sectoral balance sheets,[73]

---

[72]National financial systems are subject to threats from internal conditions and external shocks. This section does not cover statistical issues and MPIs related to external shocks because they have already been discussed extensively in the work leading up to the development of the data template on international reserves and foreign currency liquidity. See IMF (1999d).

[73]See Inter-Secretariat Working Group on National Accounts (1993). Financial accounts within the System of National Accounts, 1993 (SNA93) framework include detailed flow of funds accounts (Tables 11.3a, 11.3b), balance sheets and accumulation accounts (Table 13.2), and stocks of financial assets and liabilities analyzed by debtor and creditor (Tables 13.3a, 13.3b). Although few countries will compile these accounts at the level of detail presented in SNA93, the accounts have the flexibility to be focused on analytical or policy questions important to each country while still retaining consistency with the overall framework and international comparability.

can provide the detailed financial information for the financial sector and other sectors of the economy that can be used for macroprudential analysis. Among the numerous MPIs that can be constructed directly from monetary statistics or other financial macrostatistical frameworks are: central bank credit to banks, the ratio of deposits to M2, the ratio of loans to capital, the ratio of loans to total deposits, lending to nonresidents, the ratio of foreign currency loans to total loans, the ratio of foreign currency liabilities to total capital, and the distribution of credit by sector.

International standards exist for the construction of these macrostatistics frameworks, which contribute to their comparability across countries. An important attribute of these frameworks is that they present specific sectors within the context of the overall economy and can be used to analyze the dynamics of the financial sector and the transmission of financial stress across sectors. Also, these frameworks are flexible and can be enhanced with additional detail needed for macroprudential analysis. These frameworks are highly developed in only a few countries.

The IMF is moving to promote compilation of financial sector macroeconomic statistics harmonized with international standards through the forthcoming *Monetary and Financial Statistics Manual*. Financial statistics compiled in accordance with the manual can be further augmented to provide more macroprudential information, such as on impairment of claims, credit concentration, maturity of liabilities, subordinated debt, capital adequacy, connected lending, and relations with foreign affiliates.[74] Work is currently ongoing also at the ECB to augment the monetary statistics program with macroprudential information (see Appendix I).

Aggregations of Microprudential Data

The second major type of information used for macroprudential analysis consists of summations of information used by supervisors to assess the condition of individual banks. In addition to the use of these data in specific MPIs, a recent report by the Bank of England called for national supervisory authorities to design a template with minimum requirements for key indicators of bank quality for disclosure of aggregated microprudential data to the public:

We recommend that national supervisory agencies take upon themselves the responsibility for the collection, compilation and dissemination of data on banks to meet the needs of users. These data would be at least at the peer group and aggregate level; both on solo and consolidated basis; and include key indicators of capital, asset quality, earnings and liquidity, such as capital adequacy ratios, non-performing loans as a percentage of total assets, return on assets and equity, and a breakdown of assets and liabilities by maturity. Data should be published on a quarterly frequency. The above list is only a suggested bare minimum and not a comprehensive list of indicators. A common disclosure template in the form of a minimum requirement could be agreed on by the Basel Committee on Banking Supervision and could be so designed to meet the needs of macroprudential surveillance. This would require implementation of greater disclosure requirements than those currently applicable in many countries, and possibly even legislative changes to augment the authority of supervisors to ask for and to publish these data. We recommend that countries take up this task with the priority it deserves.[75]

Some microprudential information can be meaningfully aggregated to provide a useful depiction of the condition of the financial sector. Some other microprudential information, however, may reflect specific information needs of supervisors on the condition of individual banks that might prove difficult to aggregate or unsuitable for aggregation. For example, VaR analysis is only valid for the analysis of specific portfolios. Other potential MPIs are affected in a similar way. Also, simple aggregation of prudential information of individual banks can disguise important structural information, and it is often necessary to supplement the aggregate data with information on dispersion, peer-group analysis, and the interrelationships between systemically large banks.

It is instructive to review how the most commonly used indicator, the risk-based capital ratio, could be aggregated into a statistic to describe the condition of the banking sector. The ratios for individual banks cannot be directly aggregated—data on the numerator (capital) and the denominator (risk-adjusted assets) must be collected from each bank and separately aggregated. The supervisory definition of capital used as the numerator is unique so that data cannot be extracted directly from either accounting records or statistical sources, and there are analytical needs to compile separate information on the three tiers of capital recognized by supervisors. Likewise, data on risk-

---

[74]A number of MPIs can be drawn directly from the financial balance sheet data used in the forthcoming *Monetary and Financial Statistics Manual*. An advantage of collecting MPIs through use of a standard framework is that macroprudential information will apply common statistical standards, such as a standard statistical definition of residency, which helps integrate the macroprudential information into an economywide statistical setting.

[75]See Davis, Hamilton, Heath, Mackie, and Narain (1999), p. 83.

weighted assets used in the denominator are also based on supervisory concepts not used in accounting or statistical work, and thus are not comparable across countries because they are affected by national accounting practices for valuation of assets, accrual of interest, and recognition of impairment. The aggregate ratio is calculated by simple division of the aggregate numerator by the aggregate denominator. A low ratio is a clear sign of vulnerability, and a declining trend may signal increased risk exposure and possible capital adequacy problems. A relatively high ratio, however, does not guarantee that there are not serious difficulties in financial institutions that account for a significant share of the system's assets.

There have been numerous calls for compilation and dissemination of information on the aggregate risk-based capital ratio but, as described above, a number of practical and conceptual issues, and decisions about ancillary information, need to be considered in creating a statistical measure of the ratio.

Statistical Issues Affecting MPIs and International Comparability

Table 4 summarizes some of the major statistical issues affecting MPIs.[76] This table cross-classifies selected MPIs by major types of issues that could impede their construction, affect their usefulness for analysis or disclosure, or affect international comparability. The focus is on issues related to compilation of MPIs constructed from aggregated individual bank prudential data, which—in contrast to financial macrostatistics, for which there are recognized international standards—are often affected by a range of statistical problems that might impair their comparability across countries and reliability as indicators. Even where ample individual bank prudential data exist, there might be practical difficulties or conceptual problems in compiling them into statistical aggregates. The most important statistical issues are discussed in the following subsections.

Absence or Diversity of Standards

The usefulness of MPIs for surveillance and public disclosure is hindered by incomparability across countries because of a lack of international standards, highly diverse national standards, failure of standards to keep up with rapid innovation in financial markets, or failure to adhere to applicable prudential or accounting standards. In the cases of supervisory and accounting standards, there may be no applicable international standards, or highly diverse national standards may exist. Also, existing accounting standards in many countries often apply historical valuations to claims and liabilities, which can disguise changes in corporations' financial conditions. Little or no work has been done to date to develop statistical formulas and definitions for most of the proposed MPIs.

Poor Data on Asset Quality

Poor information on asset quality and on the holders of weak credits impairs the analysis of risks facing the financial sector by reducing the usefulness of balance sheet data for making assessments of the conditions of financial institutions. These data limitations often can hide the buildup of systemic financial sector problems. Specific data limitations include lack of complete or realistic information on the full recoverable value of loans and securities, country risk, foreign exchange risk, exposures by counterparties, and the nettability of claims.[77]

Use of National Versus Global Consolidations

Much supervisory data is collected using a global consolidation that incorporates the worldwide activity of a bank into a single financial statement, which guarantees that all of its relevant activity is captured. Such data, however, might relate only loosely to financial conditions within any specific country in which a multinational firm operates, and much of the reported data may refer to activity or financial positions outside national authorities' jurisdictions and policy control. In contrast, standard macroeconomic statistics use a national consolidation, and therefore exclude affiliated units in other countries.[78] National financial statistics can be related to the other national macroeconomic statistics, such as GDP or national interest rates, and cover national financial activity that will be under the influence of national policy officials.

---

[76]Table 4 covers MPIs closely related to the banking sector. Statistical needs for MPIs extend over nonbank financial institutions, securities markets, and nonfinancial corporations, but data outside the banking sector are often less available. Furthermore, the table provides only a first cut at identifying specific statistical problems. The survey of country practices will help identify more precisely the types of problems that exist and their severity.

[77]Netting refers to legal and supervisory procedures that permit gross claims and liabilities between two institutions to be netted into a single asset or liability position.

[78]For example, data based on a national consolidation exclude the foreign currency exposures of a bank's subsidiaries located in other countries. In contrast, such information is captured within the global consolidation used by supervisors in order to cover the resources and risks to the entire bank.

Table 4. Statistical Issues Affecting MPIs

	No Prudential Standards	No Statistical Standards	Diverse Accounting Standards	Consolidation Issues	Poor Data on Asset Quality	Bank-Specific Information	Derivatives Issues
Capital adequacy indicators							
Aggregate capital adequacy ratios	•	•	•	•	•	•	
Distribution of the capital adequacy ratios	•	•	n.a.	•	n.a.	•	
Asset quality indicators							
Lending institution							
Sectoral credit concentration	•	•	•	•	•	•	•
Ratio of foreign currency loans to total loans	•	•	•	•	•	•	•
Ratio of nonperforming loans and provisions to total loans	•	•	•	•	•		•
Loans to unprofitable public sector entities	•	•	•	•	•		n.a.
Provisions for nonperforming loans	•	•	•	•	•		n.a.
Risk profile of assets	•	•	•	•	•	•	
Ratio of connected lending to total lending	•	•	•				n.a.
Ratio of loans to capital (leverage ratio)	•	•	•	•	•		n.a.
Delays in payments	•	•	•	•	•		•
Borrowing institution							
Debt-equity ratios		•	•	•	•	n.a.	•
Corporate profitability	n.a.	•	•	•	•	n.a.	•
Other indicators of corporate conditions	n.a.	n.a.	n.a.	n.a.	n.a.	n.a.	n.a.
Household indebtedness	•	•	•	•	•	n.a.	n.a.
Management indicators							
Ratio of expenses to total revenue	•	•	•	•	•	•	•
Earnings per employee		•					•
Number of newly licensed institutions	n.a.	n.a.	n.a.	n.a.	n.a.	n.a.	n.a.
Profitability indicators							
Ratio of net profits to assets	•	•	•	•	•	n.a.	•
Ratio of net profits to equity	•	•	•	•	•	n.a.	•
Ratio of net interest income to income/assets	•	•	•	•			
Ratio of operating expenditure to income/assets	•	•	•	•			•
Narrow customer base	n.a.		n.a.	n.a.	n.a.	n.a.	n.a.
Interest rate spreads	n.a.	•	n.a.	•	n.a.	•	n.a.
Liquidity indicators							
Central bank credit to financial institutions	•	•	•	•	•	n.a.	
Deposits relative to monetary aggregates	n.a.	•	n.a.	n.a.	n.a.	n.a.	n.a.
Segmentation of interbank rates	•	•	n.a.	n.a.	n.a.	•	n.a.
Ratio of loans to noninterbank deposits	•	•	•	•	•		
Ratio of liquid assets to total assets (liquidity ratios)	•	•	•	•	•		
Maturity structure of assets and liabilities	•	•	n.a.				•
Secondary market liquidity	n.a.	•	n.a.	n.a.	n.a.	n.a.	n.a.

Sensitivity to market risk indicators						
Ratio of net foreign exchange exposure to capital	•		•	•	•	•
Average interest repricing periods, assets and liabilities	•	n.a.	•	•	•	
Average duration for assets and liabilities	•	n.a.	n.a.	•	•	
Ratio of equity exposure to capital	•	•	•	n.a.	n.a.	
Ratio of commodity price exposure to capital	•	•	n.a.	n.a.	n.a.	
Market-based indicators						
Stock market prices	n.a.	n.a.	n.a.	n.a.	n.a.	n.a.
Excess yields	n.a.	•	•	•	•	
Credit ratings	•				•	
Sovereign yield spreads	•	n.a.	n.a.	n.a.	n.a.	

Notes: Types of statistical issues identified:

No prudential standards. Indicates that international supervisory or regulatory standards do not exist for these MPIs or for key components of the MPIs. For example, the absence of uniform supervisory standards for provisions or accruals of income on impaired loans could result in wide variations in the meaning of MPIs employing information on the value of loans or bank profitability. Therefore, data reported by national authorities may employ different concepts or compilation methods and might be incomparable across countries.

No statistical standards. Indicates that international statistical standards have not been promulgated for these MPIs or for key components of the MPIs, or that statistical equivalents to supervisory concepts have not yet been developed. For example, in the first case, there are no statistical standards on accruals of income on impaired loans. In the second case, little work has been done to date to develop standard statistical measures to capture supervisory information, even for straightforward measures such as sectoral concentration of lending.

Diverse accounting standards. Indicates that an MPI is unlikely to be comparable across countries because of diverse accounting practices in different countries.

Consolidation issues. Indicates that the consolidation used by a bank can affect the meaning of the MPI. Most important, supervisory information collected from a multinational bank using a worldwide consolidation that encompasses activity throughout the world might have little relevance for the analysis of the condition of the financial sector in specific countries in which the bank operates. Consolidation issues may also arise because of variations between countries in the units consolidated within the reports (holding companies, foreign trade subsidiaries).

Poor data on asset quality. Refers to poor or missing information on the quality of assets, such as impairment of claims, misreporting of the effective value of claims, excessive volatility of assets, country risk, or risks from overconcentration of investments.

Bank-specific information. Refers to prudential information specific to individual banks that cannot plausibly be aggregated to provide information on the overall financial sector. Qualitative information, such as information on the skills and background of management, which is information typically sought by supervisors, cannot be aggregated. Moreover, information related to specific portfolios held by banks (VaR, net foreign exchange exposure) often cannot be aggregated, or must be used in conjunction with dispersion indices or measures of concentration.

Derivatives issues. Refers to issues related to the recognition, valuation, or accounting treatment of derivatives and off-balance sheet instruments.

The use of the two different consolidations can have important implications for the construction of MPIs. For example, a global risk-based capital ratio is relevant for the supervision of a bank operating in multiple countries, but it is not possible to aggregate meaningfully global ratios for all banks operating in a country. This implies that there is a need to collect separate data for institutions' domestic activity and their global activity. Such a separation is straightforward for some assets and liabilities, such as loans and deposits, but for other items there may be difficulties such as uncertainty over the allocation to individual national branches of capital items registered at the level of the global corporation.[79]

The scope of MPIs in different countries can also differ significantly depending on the precise collection of units drawn within the consolidated reports. This scope, in turn, depends on factors such as national legal definitions, the scope of activities permitted by banks, and rules on consolidation of subsidiaries and branches. Moreover, a related statistical coverage problem is that rapid change in financial markets can result in growth of new financial industries that might not be captured within existing supervisory or statistical reporting systems. A particular concern is that supervisory or statistical systems may fail to encompass all financial activities that might involve significant systemic risks (e.g., hedge funds and other mutual funds, consumer finance companies, trust funds, securities clearing systems).

Derivatives and Off-Balance Sheet Positions

Financial derivatives and off-balance sheet positions present special problems in evaluating the condition of financial institutions, because of the lack of reporting of positions, high volatility, and potentially large positions. Such concerns have led the accounting profession to move toward explicit recognition of virtually all derivatives on balance sheets using a market value or equivalent measure of value (fair value). International statistical standards for recognition and valuation of derivatives have also been developed, largely based on work at the IMF. These standards are now just beginning to be implemented, mostly in the context of the Economic and Monetary Union (EMU) monetary statistics and the international reserves template. The Basel Committee on

Banking Supervision, of BIS, and IOSCO have also proposed new standards for the recognition, valuation, and disclosure of information on derivatives.[80] Increased recognition of most derivatives on balance sheets at fair value, which is in line with most new regulatory proposals, will affect many of the proposed MPIs.

Options for Further Development of MPIs

A precondition for further work on aggregation of prudential information for individual banks is ascertaining through surveys or other means the feasibility (given national legal and supervisory practices and statistical operations) of collecting data for the various types of MPIs that have been proposed. Because of the diversity in national supervisory practices and philosophies of supervision, the types of prudential data collected by national central banks and national supervisory offices are not well known. The IMF is therefore in the process of carrying out a survey of national authorities and users of MPIs to ascertain what types of MPIs they need, whether prudential statistics are compiled systematically for individual banks or are available as aggregates, the types of data covered, gaps in coverage, and the accounting, legal, and institutional standards that affect compilation of the data. National practices and regulations related to public disclosure are also being assessed. An important aspect of the survey is to gather information and ascertain the feasibility of constructing a core set of indicators or whether different sets of MPIs are required for different types of economies—such as financial centers, other industrial economies, emerging market economies, and developing economies.

The survey and technical reviews are aimed at gaining a clear understanding of what is involved in compiling or disseminating MPIs. For example, it might be found that a significant number of MPIs are inherently microeconomic in nature and cannot be meaningfully aggregated. Moreover, new MPIs might be proposed and the priorities in the formulation of international standards might change.[81]

---

[79]In general, it might be difficult to assess the condition of the capital account of national branches of global enterprises because of difficulty in allocating the strengths or weaknesses of the global capital account to individual branches. There might also be a lack of transparency on the allocation of income or expenses on collaborative work between branches in different countries.

[80]In September 1998, the Basel Committee on Banking Supervision and the IOSCO Technical Committee issued a joint report that covers minimum information standards on credit, liquidity, market, and earnings risk that require marked-to-market and notional value data on derivatives by counterparty, maturity, and type of underlying risk; see BIS and IOSCO (1998). The report also suggests that supervisors have access to institutions' internal VaR estimates.

[81]For example, the Basel Committee on Banking Supervision has proposed a substantial revision of the risk-based capital ratio.

Another important element in developing MPIs is to consider them in the context of the rapid changes in perspectives and standards of supervisors, accountants, and the public. Many initiatives are under way to develop standards that might bring about greater coherence and enhance the quality of MPIs.[82] Important changes in standards are now taking place and others are forthcoming in a process that may take considerable time to approach completion. As standards are developed, national practices will gradually come into line, which should enhance reporting within each country and improve the international comparability of data. Moreover, to the extent that standard-setting organizations come to agreement among themselves (including on the adoption of applicable international statistical standards), the results will be greater coherence in compiled data, better understanding by the public, improved statistical support for the development of policy, and reductions in respondents' and compilers' costs of compiling data. Substantial differences across countries will continue for some time though, which requires an approach that works in parallel, both for greater future harmonization of data, but that also proceeds now on the basis of available, unharmonized data.

In summary, additional information gathering and technical research is needed before we come to a decision point on the statistical strategies to follow in developing MPIs. Depending on options selected for developing MPIs, major resource and prioritization issues as well as organizational or legal issues could confront international organizations and national entities. Some types of MPIs may prove difficult and costly to compile, or may require new data collection systems that do not fit easily into existing statistical arrangements. Conversely, much of the work of upgrading statistical systems to encompass MPIs dovetails with the ongoing work at the IMF and elsewhere to enhance statistical, accounting, auditing, and supervisory systems to keep pace with globalization and rapid changes in financial markets,[83] and thus might be viewed as incremental initiatives to work already under way.

Following is a list of some of the statistical options available for compiling MPIs. The specific strategy for following these options will depend greatly on the willingness, technical strengths, and resources of the various international and national entities that might be involved.

(1) Monetary statistics could be augmented with specific types of data used for macroprudential analysis. The additional data sought would consist mostly of balance sheet information, but might also include information on financial institutions' income, expenses, and profitability. Under this option, the IMF would augment its existing system for compiling monetary statistics and use it as a basis for compiling MPIs across a range of countries.[84]

(2) A new monthly or quarterly compilation of financial sector prudential data could be instituted, covering all MPIs (should a decision be made not to use option 1), or covering only those MPIs that are not readily included within a monetary statistics framework. The lead role in such work could be taken by the IMF or other international organizations.

(3) National entities could be encouraged to compile and disseminate unharmonized national data on the condition of individual banks or aggregations of microprudential data.

(4) National entities could enhance their programs to compile financial macrostatistics, especially sectoral balance sheets and flow of funds accounts, to support macroprudential analysis. These accounts are tools to assess the financial strength or vulnerabilities of the major sectors of an economy and the potential for transmission of financial stress between sectors.

---

[82]Important work on the development of standards is being undertaken by the Basel Committee on Banking Supervision, IOSCO, the International Accounting Standards Committee, international statistical organizations, regional organizations, and national supervisors, among others. An important initiative affecting MPIs was the enactment in early 1999 of *International Accounting Standard No. 39—Financial Instruments: Recognition and Measurement*, which mandates that virtually all financial positions be recorded on balance sheet at market value or equivalent and that impairment and loss of market value be reported on an ongoing basis. This standard, where implemented by national authorities, would markedly improve the usefulness of accounting data in the construction of MPIs by providing an accurate and timely depiction of the value of financial institutions' portfolios. The International Accounting Standards are general standards, however, which may be implemented in somewhat different ways in different countries. An important adjunct of this work is the cooperation of the International Accounting Standards Committee with IOSCO to extend standards to cover reporting and valuation of securities.

---

[83]This fluidity also offers the potential for modification and upgrading of accounting, auditing, supervisory, or statistical standards to better extract macroprudential information and to solidify their methodological bases so that MPIs can be soundly constructed and made comparable across countries. Achieving such improvements will require close cooperation between statistical, accounting, and supervisory authorities.

[84]This option has similarities to the ECB's program of collecting MPI information for the EU and its member countries via its monetary statistics compilation system (see Appendix I).

(5) Modalities for monitoring or contributing to ongoing work to develop international standards could be explored. One possibility would be to convene an interdisciplinary working group that would follow proposals for accounting, auditing, supervisory, and statistical standards as well as changes in disclosure requirements for financial institutions, and that would support harmonization with international statistical standards.

(6) A handbook or manual on statistical compilation of MPIs could be prepared to provide guidance to compilers and to assist users in analyzing MPIs.

VII   Macroprudential Indicators and Data Dissemination

This section reviews issues related to the public dissemination of MPIs, in recognition of their crucial role in the strengthening of financial sector surveillance and the oversight of the global financial system. It discusses insights from IMF approaches to the data dissemination standards, taking into account the conclusions of the September 1999 consultative meeting on member countries' and other experiences in MPI identification and dissemination.

The identification of a core set of MPIs is seen as one of the prerequisites for dissemination of MPIs to the general public. The core MPIs would have to fulfill the following criteria: (1) usefulness in financial systems surveillance; (2) comparability across countries; (3) feasibility of collecting harmonized data; and (4) existence of "best practices" with regard to coverage, periodicity, and timeliness of the data that are being disseminated. Given the substantial work ahead in crafting a core set of MPIs, participants at the meeting believed it was premature at this time to recommend specific modalities for dissemination of MPIs, but supported the development of incentives to national authorities to compile and disseminate them.

IMF Initiatives in Data Dissemination Standards

The SDDS and the General Data Dissemination System (GDDS) embody a structured approach to encourage data dissemination.[85] The SDDS has operated since 1996 as a system of well-defined guidelines—that is, a standard—for countries to provide the public with comprehensive, timely, reliable, and accessible macroeconomic data.[86] In order to meet the

standard, the SDDS countries have made significant improvements in their practices for the compilation and dissemination of the SDDS data categories and underlying databases.

Whereas the SDDS is intended for countries that are actively involved in international capital markets, or that aspire to do so, and that have relatively well-developed statistical systems, the GDDS serves as a framework for the long-term improvement of data and statistical practices across the wider IMF membership. At the time the SDDS was initiated, its requirements were recognized as very demanding and not necessarily applicable or relevant for all countries. Consequently, it was agreed that the GDDS be created to provide a vehicle to support improvements in the statistical capacity of the remainder of the membership. The GDDS was established in 1997.

Lessons from the SDDS and GDDS

Three lessons can be drawn from the SDDS and GDDS approach:

(1) The SDDS may be viewed as successful because it continues to provide incentives for countries to improve their practices on compiling and disseminating macroeconomic data. Countries are aware that subscribing to the SDDS may be viewed by market participants as highly desirable and could enhance their ratings on the international capital markets.

(2) The prescriptions contained in the SDDS have been developed based on evidence of best or preferred practices in the compilation and dissemination of macroeconomic data by coun-

---

[85]They also complement other initiatives undertaken by the IMF to foster macroeconomic stability and financial system soundness through enhanced transparency, such as the development of the *Code of Good Practices on Transparency in Monetary and Financial Policies* and the *Code of Good Practices on Fiscal Transparency*.

[86]In subscribing to the SDDS, countries commit to bringing their national statistical practices into alignment with the SDDS

requirements for data coverage, periodicity, timeliness, access practices (including data release calendars), integrity, and quality proxies (including summary methodologies). Through the Dissemination Standards Bulletin Board (DSBB), SDDS subscribers provide information about their statistical practices (so-called metadata) for a total of 20 macroeconomic categories, as well as access to actual data. The SDDS countries post at least the two latest data observations for each SDDS data category on their national summary data page to which the DSBB is electronically linked. The DSBB website is http://dsbb.imf.org.

tries that participate in financial markets or that aspire to do so.

(3) The establishment of two parallel tracks for work on data dissemination standards—SDDS and GDDS—entails a recognition of the different stages of development of countries' statistical systems and the need for an approach to dissemination standards that takes this reality into account.

Conclusions on Dissemination Issues from the Consultative Meeting

The major conclusions on data dissemination reached by the participants of the consultative meeting can be summarized as follows:[87]

- There is no single set of MPIs that is currently being disseminated by many countries or that is seen as superior to others, nor are there clearly identifiable best practices with regard to the dissemination of MPI data.

- In the absence of a consensus concerning a core set of MPIs, it is premature to decide whether MPIs should be included in the SDDS or along other tracks for promoting dissemination.

- Differences in approaches to the degree of disseminating data, maintaining confidentiality, and providing assessments on the condition of the banking sector often seem to be based on different perceptions of how markets might react to this information. Some authorities fear that markets might react adversely to "bad" news about banking sector soundness. The "bad" news could be either perceived or officially validated by authorities' assessments. Other countries disseminate a wide range of macroprudential indicators in the belief that these data would enable the markets to make the right decisions.[88]

- Participants agreed on the need for an effort at greater harmonization of data in terms of coverage, periodicity, timeliness, and public access.

- The meeting supported conducting a survey of national supervisors, statistical authorities, and users to evaluate the prospects for compiling and disseminating MPIs.

Next Steps

MPI Dissemination Standards

Dissemination standards typically evolve based on evidence of best practices that are comparable across countries.[89] It is clear that significant work lies ahead in developing such good practices for MPIs, but also that it should take place in conjunction with progress in identifying a core set of MPIs for financial system surveillance, as well as in resolving the statistical issues of measurement.

Actual practice (still to be further investigated) may demonstrate (1) that certain MPIs are more relevant for a particular country or country-group and less for another, and (2) that countries differ in their statistical capabilities to collect reliable, frequent, and timely data on MPIs.

The current SDDS would perhaps provide a solution to the first situation by means of its "as relevant" provisions that exempt countries from certain requirements that may not be relevant for a country's particular economic structure. In such cases, the country must make these differences transparent by providing explicit information in the metadata explaining how and why the particular data set is not considered to be relevant for the country's economy.

As for the second situation, the case could be made for a differentiated approach to eventual MPI dissemination—for example, along the lines of the two tiers represented by the SDDS and the GDDS.

Incentives

Incentives for the authorities to disseminate reliable and timely MPIs could come from different sources. Among these are international technical assistance to improve the collection and compilation of MPIs, and the "appeal" of a technical standard in which MPIs might be included.

With regard to the appeal of a standard, it should be noted that eventually including MPIs in the existing SDDS as a dynamic, evolving standard could have the following benefits: (1) further strengthening the role of the SDDS; (2) leveraging the "good will" of the international community vis-à-vis the SDDS; (3) improving the complementarity of macroeconomic and macroprudential indicators; and (4) broadening the application of the SDDS advantages, including the provision of a comprehen-

---

[87]See Hilbers, Krueger, and Moretti (1999) for details.

[88]The basic approach taken by IMF staff—subject, of course, to concerns about confidentiality of data for individual institutions—is that information is a public good and that enhanced public availability of information is desirable.

[89]In contrast, in the work on international reserves and, to some extent, on external debt in the SDDS, the IMF took the lead in "pushing the envelope" to promote increased dissemination of reliable, comprehensive, and timely data. In the case of reserves, standards were developed jointly by the IMF and a working group of the CGFS.

sive set of metadata, eventual access to data for a particular country, and facilitation of potential cross-country metadata and data comparisons.

While the SDDS is designed to evolve to meet new challenges—and has already strengthened its prescription for dissemination of data on international reserves and external debt—adding MPIs to the SDDS may result in concerns on the part of existing subscribers. This requirement was not envisaged at the time of subscription, and some countries may not be in a position to meet the MPI prescriptions, though they are otherwise in observance of the SDDS. Also, including MPIs in the SDDS could conceivably prove daunting for potential new subscribers. These various considerations do not need to be resolved now. They can be revisited later, when more of the necessary preparatory work has been undertaken.

Metadata

In light of the diverse practices in compiling MPIs and many potential statistical problems, special emphasis needs to be placed on developing a strategy regarding the role of metadata—the textual description of the data series. Information must be provided to users about the MPIs' coverage, public access, integrity of the data, and quality of the data, including compilation methods, and adherence to or departures from relevant international standards.

Appendix I Existing Data Collection Frameworks

This appendix reviews the frameworks for the collection of MPIs already in place in international and regional organizations to ascertain the types of data generally available, to identify gaps or weaknesses in coverage, and to assess the potential for exchange of data and cooperation in collection of MPIs.

International Monetary Fund

The IMF collects and disseminates a wide variety of macrostatistics, but does not systematically collect financial microdata. The IMF's monetary statistics comprise a very extensive database on banking institutions. These data are potentially very important for macroprudential analysis because many MPIs and the monetary statistics compiled by the IMF are derived from the same data sources—central bank and commercial bank balance sheets. The data have a monthly periodicity and are provided to the IMF as soon as possible after the reference date. An analytical presentation of monetary data is published in *International Financial Statistics*. The published data only highlight a limited number of monetary and credit aggregates. These aggregates are presented in a modified balance sheet format that does not present total assets, total liabilities, and detailed capital account information, and thus does not provide the structural information needed for macroprudential analysis. Also, the monetary statistics have not been constructed under standard accounting rules, such as for valuation or provisioning, which detracts from their usefulness for macroprudential purposes. Similarly, data on bank income, expenses, and profitability, which are used in many MPIs, are not collected.

A number of changes to the methodology for compiling these monetary statistics, which will bring about greater standardization and harmonization between countries, will be introduced when the IMF's new *Manual on Monetary and Financial Statistics* is published. The manual recommends that all countries apply the statistical standards presented in the System of National Accounts, 1993, which will result in standard statistical accounting treatments, definitions of the financial sector, and classifications and treatments of financial instruments. The manual also provides for compilation of aggregate balance sheets for the domestic banking sector, which in most countries would be the only aggregate statistics on the financial positions and condition of financial institutions. Implementation of the standards in the manual would aid countries in producing MPIs in a number of ways, including by providing a framework for the classification and the measurement of financial derivatives, and recording assets at their fair market value. The framework of the manual was not designed with MPIs in mind, but it could be extended—after some conceptual work is done—to accommodate further information on MPIs, such as on asset quality, credit concentration, capital adequacy, and relations with foreign affiliates. Perhaps half of the proposed MPIs could be integrated into the monetary statistics framework, with varying degrees of difficulty.

Bank for International Settlements

The BIS publishes international banking statistics in the form of a semiannual consolidated report of statistics on the amount, maturity, and sectoral and nationality distribution of international bank lending. These data are available to the public through the BIS website (http://www.bis.org). The data are also included in a joint BIS/IMF/OECD/World Bank quarterly statistical release on external debt, which was recently introduced in order to facilitate timely access to a single set of debt indicators. These data are also analyzed in depth in the BIS *International Banking and Financial Market Developments*, which also presents discussions of conceptual and statistical issues related to the data, as needed.

The BIS staff, partly in support of the Committee on the Global Financial System and its predecessor, the Euro-Currency Standing Committee, have carried out work following the financial crises in the early 1990s with a view to identifying indicators of financial risk, and data have been collected as needed to support these analyses.

European Central Bank

The ECB has initiated an MPI project that has identified the EMU monetary statistics as a source of macroprudential information. The EMU countries compile a harmonized set of monetary statistics to provide the statistical basis for the operation of the EMU single monetary policy.[90] The statistics are compiled on a timely basis according to statistical standards based on the European System of Accounts, 1995 (ESA95).[91] Because universal banking prevails in Europe, the EMU monetary data cover most of the EMU financial sector.

The EMU monetary statistics are presented in a straightforward balance sheet format, with a reasonable amount of detail on financial instruments and counterparty sector. The data compiled for each country cover each institution's activity within the country, and separate information is provided on positions with other countries within the EMU and with nonresidents of the EMU. This statistical construction permits the European System of Central Banks (ESCB) to produce a comprehensive picture of the financial positions of domestic financial institutions vis-à-vis residents of the country and residents of the EMU. Although there are some limitations to the data because the reporting system was designed primarily to serve monetary statistics purposes, the EMU monetary statistics framework is comprehensive and methodologically strong. The framework is also being enhanced to better incorporate the needs of macroprudential analysis.

The Banking Supervision Committee of the ESCB has initiated a project to identify MPIs for the EU banking sector, and has established a Working Group on Macroprudential Analysis to that end (see Section IV). The ECB has recently completed a "gaps exercise" to inquire about the availability of data at the EU national central banks needed to calculate MPIs from existing data sources. A selection has been made of indicators to follow and data sources to use. The ECB and national central banks are now putting into place mechanisms for compiling the data. Most of the balance sheet data sought will be taken directly from monetary statistics: monthly balance sheets for the banking sector, supplemented by quarterly information that provides greater detail on borrowing from and lending to nonbank financial institutions, corporations, and households (including a split between consumer credit and mortgage lending). There is also information on particular types of lending, deposit rates, and interest rate spreads. Data collection at this stage is limited to the banking sector. In addition to the collection of data through the monetary statistics system, other data are being gathered from national supervisory sources within the Banking Supervision Committee. This exercise draws also on data collection carried out in other supervisory forums, notably the "Groupe de Contact" (composed of representatives of the supervisory authorities of the countries in the European Economic Area). Subsequent actions will depend on the results of the exercise.

EMU member countries also prepare financial accounts that detail financial assets and liabilities of all major sectors of an economy, and the ECB and Eurostat jointly prepare the Monetary Union Financial Accounts (MUFA). The statistical standards for financial accounts are based on ESA95 and thus are harmonized with the standards for monetary statistics, so that it is possible to embed the analysis of the banking sector within the statistical framework for financial activity for the entire economy and its key components. The specific importance of financial accounts for MPIs is that relationships between the financial sector and its creditor and debtor sectors are made explicit in a way that allows tracking of the influence of macroeconomic trends on the condition of the financial sector. The sectoral accounts also permit analysis of the financial strength or vulnerabilities of the various sectors, thus supporting the analysis of transmission of financial strains between the rest of the economy and the banking sector.

World Bank

As noted in Section IV, the World Bank is involved in the analysis of financial sector soundness, including through its joint work with the IMF under the FSAP. The Financial Sector Liaison Committee of the World Bank and the IMF is currently discussing options for the joint development of a financial sector database for internal use that will include qualitative information, macroeconomic time series, and aggregated microprudential information. Most of the statistical data will be drawn from databases maintained by other institutions, but will also include information gathered during the FSAP missions and other consultations with member countries. The World Bank also makes use of macroprudential information in risk assessment models used in conjunction with its lending operations.

---

[90]EU countries that are not members of the EMU are required to use many of the same statistical standards as the EMU countries.

[91]The ESA95 standards closely conform with the standards in the IMF's forthcoming *Monetary and Financial Statistics Manual*.

Organization for Economic Cooperation and Development

The OECD collects a wide range of financial sector data from its member countries for use in its regular analysis of national and international financial conditions, as presented in its *Financial Market Trends* and numerous other analytical and statistical reports. The OECD does not presently collect specific MPIs, but uses a broad range of macro- and microstatistics and qualitative information in its assessments of countries' financial situations. However, two OECD publications are of particular interest for macroprudential purposes.

- *Bank Profitability* presents data on (1) bank income, expenditure, and profitability; (2) balance sheets, with substantial detail; (3) capital adequacy; (4) supplemental data on the number of institutions and employment; and (5) some limited information on the overall structure of the financial system. A number of countries provide data disaggregated by major type of bank. Data are available for all OECD member countries, using a standard set of tables that have a rather detailed breakdown. The data are subject to a number of limitations, however, mostly the result of diversity in national coverage.[92] Data

have an annual periodicity, and the latest data in the 1999 report are from 1997 for all but a few countries.

- *Financial Accounts of OECD Countries* presents standard tables with annual data on flows of funds and balance sheets of most OECD countries. Detail is given by type of financial instrument and counterparty sector, and sometimes with links to gross saving and investment in the national accounts. These data are compiled in accordance with SNA standards and thus provide links between the financial sector and the overall national economy. This multisector by financial instrument framework is potentially useful for macroprudential analysis by permitting examination of the concentration of lending by sector and the transmission of financial stress across sectors. Although adherence to SNA standards imparts some comparability of data across countries, the foreword warns that the "extreme diversity that characterizes the financial institutions of the member countries and the financial instruments they use may limit the comparability of the statistics." Data users are advised to refer to a methodological supplement for information on standard concepts, calculation methods, and individual country notes. Other limitations are the restricted country coverage, availability of only annual data, and the long lags in the production of data by some countries.

---

[92]"The institutional coverage of the tables has been largely dictated by the availability of data on income and expenditure accounts of banks. As a result of the reporting methods used in OECD countries, the tables are not integrated in the system of national accounts and are, therefore, not compatible with the financial accounts of OECD countries. International comparisons in the field of income and expenditure accounts of banks are particularly difficult because of considerable differences in OECD countries regarding structural and regulatory features of national

banking systems, accounting rules and practices, and reporting methods." (Organization for Economic Cooperation and Development, 1999, Foreword).

Appendix II   Special Data Dissemination Standard and General Data Dissemination System

Recent financial crises have given rise to increased efforts by the international community to foster macroeconomic stability and financial system soundness. Transparency in the functioning of world capital markets and of countries' financial policies is being promoted. The IMF has taken numerous steps to enhance transparency and openness, including the establishment and recent strengthening of disclosure standards to guide countries in a number of areas, including data dissemination. The need for these standards, first highlighted by the Mexican financial crisis in 1994/95, was underscored by the recent financial crises in Asia and elsewhere. The Special Data Dissemination Standard, complete with an electronic bulletin board—and in a growing number of cases, electronic links that enable users to move between the metadata and the actual data—has been in place since March 1996. The General Data Dissemination System was established in December 1997.

Special Data Dissemination Standard

Countries subscribing to the SDDS undertake to follow good practices in four dimensions:

- Data—coverage, periodicity, and timeliness;
- Access by the public—dissemination of advance release calendars, and simultaneous release of the data;
- Integrity—disclosure of information on laws governing the compilation and release of the data, access to the data by other government officials prior to release, ministerial commentary accompanying the release of the data, revision policy, and advance notice of major changes in methodology; and
- Quality—dissemination of documentation on methodology and sources, and dissemination of detailed data that support statistical cross-checks.

Under the SDDS, data dissemination practices are described for a total of 20 data categories cover-

ing the real, fiscal, financial, and external sectors as well as for population, and are posted on the Dissemination Standards Bulletin Board. To date, 47 countries—representing a mix of industrial, emerging market, and transition economies—have voluntarily subscribed to the SDDS. Countries are also required to establish an Internet site containing the actual data disseminated under the SDDS, called a national summary data page that is hyperlinked to the DSBB.

The SDDS has led to wider availability and enhanced timeliness of published data and greater use of advance data release calendars. In light of the recent financial crises, the IMF has also taken steps to strengthen the SDDS, particularly in the areas of international reserves and external debt. The new reserves template is more comprehensive than the existing prescription, with subscribers having until March 31, 2000, to meet the new requirements. Improvements in external debt data are also taking place.

General Data Dissemination System

The GDDS, like the SDDS, was developed in close collaboration with a wide range of producers and users of statistics. The primary focus of the GDDS is on improvement in data quality. This stands in contrast with the SDDS, where the focus is on dissemination in countries that generally already meet high data quality standards. Against this background, the GDDS is one of the most important strategic projects for the IMF in the area of statistics, where a long-standing objective has been the improvement of data and statistical practices among the membership. It is hoped that the GDDS will also be a valuable resource for bilateral and multilateral providers of technical assistance, and that the GDDS can provide the basis for enhanced cooperation with other providers of technical assistance. The GDDS's purposes are (1) to encourage member countries to improve data quality; (2) to provide a framework for evaluating needs for data improvement and setting priorities in this respect; and (3) to guide member countries in the dissemination to the public of comprehensive, timely, accessible, and reliable economic, financial, and sociodemographic statistics. The framework takes into account, across the broad range of countries, the diversity of their economies and the developmental requirements of their statistical systems.

Dissemination Standards Bulletin Board

The DSBB website (http://dsbb.imf.org), which is maintained by the IMF, serves as a tool for market analysts and others who track economic growth, in-flation, and other economic and financial developments in countries around the world. The aim of the DSBB is to strengthen the availability of timely and comprehensive information on economic and financial statistics and to contribute to the pursuit of sound macroeconomic policies and improved functioning of financial markets.

The DSBB describes the statistical practices of the SDDS-participating countries in the collection, compilation, and dissemination of key macroeconomic indicators. DSBB users also have access to actual country data on the national summary data pages. A project is under way to enhance the DSBB website with regard to (1) presentation and functionality; (2) tools for metadata management; (3) provision of a database for data that are accessible on or via the DSBB; and (4) marketing of the DSBB.

References

Akerlof, George A., 1970, "The Market for 'Lemons': Quality Uncertainty and the Market Mechanism," *Quarterly Journal of Economics*, Vol. 84 (August), pp. 488–500.

Altman, Edward I., 1968, "Financial Ratios, Discriminant Analysis and the Prediction of Corporate Bankruptcy," *Journal of Finance,* Vol. 23 (September), pp. 589–609.

Baig, Taimur, and Ilan Goldfajn, 1999, "Financial Market Contagion in the Asian Crisis," *IMF Staff Papers*, Vol. 46 (June), pp. 167–195.

Bank for International Settlements (BIS), Basel Committee on Banking Supervision (BCBS), 1988, *International Convergence of Capital Measurement and Capital Standards* (Basel).

———, 1996, *Amendment to the Capital Accord to Incorporate Market Risks* (Basel).

———, 1997, *Principles for the Management of Interest Rate Risk* (Basel).

———, 1999a, *A New Capital Adequacy Framework* (Basel).

———, 1999b, "Capital Requirements and Bank Behaviour: The Impact of the Basel Accord," BCBS Working Paper No. 1 (Basel).

———, 1999c, "Supervisory Lessons to Be Drawn from the Asian Crisis," BCBS Working Paper No. 2 (Basel).

———, and International Organization of Securities Commissions, Technical Committee (IOSCO), 1998, *Supervisory Information Framework for Derivatives and Trading Activities* (Basel).

Bank for International Settlements, Committee on the Global Financial System, 1999, *A Review of Financial Market Events in Autumn 1998* (Basel).

Bank of England, 1999, *Financial Stability Review,* Issue 6 (London).

Berg, Andrew, and Catherine Pattillo, 1999, "Are Currency Crises Predictable?: A Test," *IMF Staff Papers*, Vol. 46 (June), pp.107–38.

Bussière, Matthieu, and Christian Mulder, 1999, "External Vulnerability in Emerging Market Economies: How High Liquidity Can Offset Weak Fundamentals and the Effects of Contagion," IMF Working Paper 99/88 (Washington: International Monetary Fund).

Caprio, Gerald, and Daniela Klingebiel, 1996, "Bank Insolvencies: Cross-Country Experience," Policy Research Working Paper No. 1620 (Washington: World Bank).

Cole, Rebel A., Barbara G. Cornyn, and Jeffrey W. Gunther, 1995, "FIMS: A New Monitoring System for Banking Institutions," *Federal Reserve Bulletin*, Vol. 81 (January), pp. 1–15.

Corsetti, Giancarlo, Paolo Pesenti, and Nouriel Roubini, 1998, "What Caused the Asian Currency and Financial Crisis? Part II: The Policy Debate," NBER Working Paper No. 6834 (Cambridge, Massachusetts: National Bureau of Economic Research).

Davis, E. Philip, 1996, "Institutional Investors, Unstable Financial Markets and Monetary Policy," in *Risk Management in Volatile Financial Markets*, ed. by Franco Bruni, Donald E. Fair, and Richard O'Brien (Boston: Kluwer Academic Publishers).

———, 1999, *Financial Data Needs for Macroprudential Surveillance—What Are the Key Indicators of Risks to Domestic Financial Stability?*, Handbooks in Central Banking, Lecture Series No. 2, Center for Central Banking Studies (London: Bank of England).

———, Robert Hamilton, Robert Heath, Fiona Mackie, and Aditya Narain, 1999, *Financial Market Data for International Financial Stability*, Center for Central Banking Studies (London: Bank of England).

Demirgüç-Kunt, Asli, and Enrica Detragiache, 1998, "The Determinants of Banking Crises in Developing and Developed Countries," *IMF Staff Papers*, Vol. 45 (March), pp. 81–109.

———, 1999, "Monitoring Banking Sector Fragility: A Multivariate Logit Approach with an Application to the 1996–97 Banking Crisis," Policy Research Working Paper No. 2085 (Washington: World Bank).

Diamond, Douglas W., and Philip H. Dybvig, 1983, "Bank Runs, Deposit Insurance, and Liquidity," *Journal of Political Economy*, Vol. 91 (June), pp. 401–19.

Dimson, Elroy, and Paul Marsh, 1997, "Stress Tests of Capital Requirements," *Journal of Banking and Finance*, Vol. 21 (December), pp. 1515–46.

Dornbusch, Rudiger, Ilan Goldfajn, and Rodrigo O. Valdés, 1995, "Currency Crises and Collapses," *Brookings Papers on Economic Activity: Macroeconomics 2*, Brookings Institution, pp. 219–94.

Downes, Patrick T., David Marston, and İnci Ötker, 1999, "Mapping Financial Sector Vulnerability in a Non-Crisis Country," IMF Policy Discussion Paper 99/4 (Washington: International Monetary Fund).

Ediz, Tolga, Ian Michael, and William Perraudin, 1998, "The Impact of Capital Requirements on U.K. Bank Behavior," *Economic Policy Review*, Federal Reserve Bank of New York, Vol. 4 (October), pp. 15–22 (London: Bank of England).

Eichengreen, Barry, and Andrew K. Rose, 1998, "Staying Afloat When the Wind Shifts: External Factors and Emerging-Market Banking Crises," NBER Working Paper No. 6370 (Cambridge, Massachusetts: National Bureau of Economic Research).

Esquivel, Gerardo, and Felipe B. Larraín, 1998, "Explaining Currency Crises," Harvard Institute for International Development, Development Discussion Paper No. 666 (Cambridge, Massachusetts: Harvard University).

Federal Deposit Insurance Corporation, 1997, *History of the Eighties: Lessons for the Future* (Washington).

Federal Reserve Bank of Kansas City, 1997, *Maintaining Financial Stability in a Global Economy: A Symposium* (Kansas City).

Fisher, Irving, 1933, "The Debt-Deflation Theory of Great Depressions," *Econometrica*, Vol. 1 (October), pp. 337–57.

Fitch IBCA, 1998, *International Bank Rating Methodology*, October 1, 1998 (New York).

Folkerts-Landau, David, and Carl-Johan Lindgren, 1998, *Toward a Framework for Financial Stability*, World Economic and Financial Surveys (Washington: International Monetary Fund).

Frankel, Jeffrey A., and Andrew K. Rose, 1996, "Currency Crashes in Emerging Markets: An Empirical Treatment," *Journal of International Economics*, Vol. 41 (November), pp. 351–66.

Fratzscher, Marcel, 1998, "Why Are Currency Crises Contagious? A Comparison of the Latin American Crisis of 1994–1995 and the Asian Crisis of 1997–1998," *Weltwirtschaftliches Archiv*, Vol. 134, No. 4, pp. 664–91.

Furman, Jason, and Joseph E. Stiglitz, 1998, "Economic Crises: Evidence and Insights from East Asia," *Brookings Papers on Economic Activity: Macroeconomics 2*, Brookings Institution, pp. 1–135.

Gavin, Michael, and Ricardo Hausmann, 1996, "The Roots of Banking Crises: The Macroeconomic Context," Inter-American Development Bank Working Paper No. 318 (Washington: Inter-American Development Bank).

Glick, Reuven, and Andrew Rose, 1998, "Contagion and Trade: Why Are Currency Crises Regional?" NBER Working Paper No. 6806 (Cambridge, Massachusetts: National Bureau of Economic Research).

Goldstein, Morris, and Philip Turner, 1996, *Banking Crises in Emerging Economies: Origins and Policy Options*, BIS Economic Paper No. 46 (Basel: Bank for International Settlements).

González-Hermosillo, Brenda, 1999, "Determinants of Ex-Ante Banking System Distress: A Macro-Micro Empirical Exploration of Some Recent Episodes," IMF Working Paper 99/33 (Washington: International Monetary Fund).

———, Ceyla Pazarbaşioğlu, and Robert Billings, 1997, "Determinants of Banking System Fragility: A Case Study of Mexico," *Staff Papers*, International Monetary Fund, Vol. 44 (September), pp. 295–314.

Goodhart, Charles, 1995, "Price Stability and Financial Fragility," in *Financial Stability in a Changing Environment*, ed. by Kuniho Sawamoto, Zenta Nakajima and Hiroo Taguchi (New York: St Martin's Press).

Guttentag, Jack, and Richard Herring, 1984, "Credit Rationing and Financial Disorder," *Journal of Finance*, Vol. 39 (December), pp. 1359–82.

Haque, Nadeem Ul, Nelson C. Mark, and Donald J. Mathieson, 1998, "The Relative Importance of Political and Economic Variables in Creditworthiness Ratings," IMF Working Paper 98/46 (Washington: International Monetary Fund).

Hardy, Daniel C., and Ceyla Pazarbaşioğlu, 1998, "Leading Indicators of Banking Crises: Was Asia Different?," IMF Working Paper 98/91 (Washington: International Monetary Fund).

Hendricks, Darryll, 1996, "Evaluation of Value-at-Risk Models Using Historical Data," *Economic Policy Review*, Federal Reserve Bank of New York, Vol. 2 (April), pp. 39–69.

Hilbers, Paul, Russell Krueger, and Marina Moretti, 1999, "Macroprudential Indicators—Seminar Discusses Ways to Assess Soundness of Financial System to Improve Surveillance," *IMF Survey*, Vol. 28, No. 18, pp. 296–97.

Honohan, Patrick, 1997, "Banking System Failures in Developing and Transition Countries: Diagnosis and Prediction," BIS Working Paper No. 39 (Basel: Bank for International Settlements).

International Monetary Fund, 1998, *World Economic Outlook: May 1998*, World Economic and Financial Surveys (Washington).

———, 1999a, "Communiqué of the Interim Committee of the Board of Governors of the International Monetary Fund," PR/99/46, September 26, 1999.

———, 1999b, *World Economic Outlook: May 1999*, World Economic and Financial Surveys (Washington).

———, 1999c, *International Capital Markets: Developments, Prospects, and Key Policy Issues*, World Economic and Financial Surveys (Washington).

———, 1999d, "Data Template on International Reserves and Foreign Currency Liquidity: Operational Guidelines," IMF Statistics Department. Available via the Internet: http://dsbb.imf.org/guide.htm.

Inter-Secretariat Working Group on National Accounts, 1993, *System of National Accounts 1993*. Prepared under the auspices of the Commission of the European Communities—Eurostat, IMF, OECD, United Nations, and World Bank (Brussels: Commission of the European Communities).

Kaminsky, Graciela, 1999, "Currency and Banking Crises: The Early Warnings of Distress," IMF Working Paper 99/178 (Washington: International Monetary Fund).

———, Saul Lizondo, and Carmen Reinhart, 1998, "Leading Indicators of Currency Crises," *IMF Staff Papers*, Vol. 45 (March), pp. 1–48.

Kaminsky, Graciela, and Carmen Reinhart, 1998, "On Crises, Contagion, and Confusion," (unpublished; Washington: George Washington University).

———, 1999, "The Twin Crises: The Causes of Banking and Balance-of-Payments Problems," *American Economic Review*, Vol. 89 (June) pp. 473–500.

Kawai, Masahiro, 1998, "The East Asian Currency Crisis: Causes and Lessons," *Contemporary Economic Policy*, Vol. 16 (April), pp. 157–72.

Keeley, Michael C., 1990, "Deposit Insurance, Risk, and Market Power in Banking," *American Economic Review,* Vol. 80 (December), pp. 1183–200.

Kodres, Laura, and Matthew Pritsker, 1998, "A Rational Expectations Model of Financial Contagion," Finance and Economics Discussion Series No. 1998–48 (Washington: Board of Governors of the Federal Reserve System).

Kwack, Sung, 1998, "The Financial Crisis in Korea: Causes and Cure," IMF Seminar Series No. 1998–19 (Washington: International Monetary Fund).

Lane, William R., Stephen W. Looney, and James W. Wansley, 1986, "An Application of the Cox Proportional Hazards Model to Bank Failure," *Journal of Banking and Finance*, Vol. 10 (December), pp. 511–31.

Lindgren, Carl-Johan, Gillian Garcia, and Matthew I. Saal, 1996, *Bank Soundness and Macroeconomic Policy* (Washington: International Monetary Fund).

Mishkin, Frederic S., 1996, "Understanding Financial Crises: A Developing Country Perspective," NBER Working Paper No. 5600 (Cambridge, Massachusetts: National Bureau of Economic Research).

Moody's Investors Service, 1999, *Bank Financial Strength Ratings* (New York).

Norges Bank, 1998, "Financial Sector Outlook: Second Half of 1998," *Economic Bulletin*, Vol. 69, Issue No. 4 (Oslo).

Organization for Economic Cooperation and Development, 1999, *Bank Profitability: Financial Statements of Banks 1999* (Paris).

Radelet, Steven, and Jeffrey D. Sachs, 1998, "The East Asian Financial Crisis: Diagnosis, Remedies, Prospects," *Brookings Papers on Economic Activity: Macroeconomic 1,* Brookings Institution, pp. 1–90.

Rojas-Suárez, Liliana, and Steven R. Weisbrod, 1995, *Financial Fragilities in Latin America: The 1980s and 1990s,* IMF Occasional Paper No. 132 (Washington: International Monetary Fund).

Sachs, Jeffrey D., Aaron Tornell, and Andrés Velasco, 1996, "Financial Crises in Emerging Markets: The Lessons from 1995," *Brookings Papers on Economic Activity: Macroeconomics 1*, Brookings Institution, pp. 147–215.

Scharfstein, David S., and Jeremy C. Stein, 1990, "Herd Behavior and Investment," *American Economic Review*, Vol. 80 (June), pp. 465–79.

Sinkey, Joseph F., 1978, "Identifying 'Problem' Banks: How Do the Banking Authorities Measure a Bank's Risk Exposure?" *Journal of Money, Credit, and Banking*, Vol. 10 (May), pp. 184–93.

Standard & Poor's, 1999, *Bank Rating Analysis Methodology Profile*, February (New York).

Sveriges Riksbank, 1999, *Financial Stability Report*, May (Stockholm).

Thomson Financial BankWatch, 1999, *BankWatch Ratings—Characteristics and Methodology* (New York).

Thomson, James B., 1991, "Predicting Bank Failures in the 1980s," *Economic Review*, Federal Reserve Bank of Cleveland, Vol. 27, No. 1, pp. 9–20.

United States, Department of the Treasury, 1999, "Statement of G-7 Finance Ministers and Central Bank Governors," LS-120, September 25, 1999.

Whalen, Gary, 1991, "A Proportional Hazards Model of Bank Failure: An Examination of Its Usefulness as an Early Warning Tool," *Economic Review,* Federal Reserve Bank of Cleveland, Vol. 27, No. 1, pp. 21–31.

Recent Occasional Papers of the International Monetary Fund

192. Macroprudential Indicators of Financial System Soundness, by a staff team led by Owen Evans, Alfredo M. Leone, Mahinder Gill, and Paul Hilbers. 2000.

191. Social Issues in IMF-Supported Programs, by Sanjeev Gupta, Louis Dicks-Mireaux, Ritha Khemani, Calvin McDonald, and Marijn Verhoeven. 2000.

190. Capital Controls: Country Experiences with Their Use and Liberalization, by Akira Ariyoshi, Karl Habermeier, Bernard Laurens, Inci Ötker-Robe, Jorge Iván Canales Kriljenko, and Andrei Kirilenko. 2000.

189. Current Account and External Sustainability in the Baltics, Russia, and Other Countries of the Former Soviet Union, by Donal McGettigan. 2000.

188. Financial Sector Crisis and Restructuring: Lessons from Asia, by Carl-Johan Lindgren, Tomás J.T. Baliño, Charles Enoch, Anne-Marie Gulde, Marc Quintyn, and Leslie Teo. 1999.

187. Philippines: Toward Sustainable and Rapid Growth, Recent Developments and the Agenda Ahead, by Markus Rodlauer, Prakash Loungani, Vivek Arora, Charalambos Christofides, Enrique G. De la Piedra, Piyabha Kongsamut, Kristina Kostial, Victoria Summers, and Athanasios Vamvakidis. 2000.

186. Anticipating Balance of Payments Crises: The Role of Early Warning Systems, by Andrew Berg, Eduardo Borensztein, Gian Maria Milesi-Ferretti, and Catherine Pattillo. 1999.

185. Oman Beyond the Oil Horizon: Policies Toward Sustainable Growth, edited by Ahsan Mansur and Volker Treichel. 1999.

184. Growth Experience in Transition Countries, 1990–98, by Oleh Havrylyshyn, Thomas Wolf, Julian Berengaut, Marta Castello-Branco, Ron van Rooden, and Valerie Mercer-Blackman. 1999.

183. Economic Reforms in Kazakhstan, Kyrgyz Republic, Tajikistan, Turkmenistan, and Uzbekistan, by Emine Gürgen, Harry Snoek, Jon Craig, Jimmy McHugh, Ivailo Izvorski, and Ron van Rooden. 1999.

182. Tax Reform in the Baltics, Russia, and Other Countries of the Former Soviet Union, by a Staff Team Led by Liam Ebrill and Oleh Havrylyshyn. 1999.

181. The Netherlands: Transforming a Market Economy, by C. Maxwell Watson, Bas B. Bakker, Jan Kees Martijn, and Ioannis Halikias. 1999.

180. Revenue Implications of Trade Liberalization, by Liam Ebrill, Janet Stotsky, and Reint Gropp. 1999.

179. Dinsinflation in Transition: 1993–97, by Carlo Cottarelli and Peter Doyle. 1999.

178. IMF-Supported Programs in Indonesia, Korea, and Thailand: A Preliminary Assessment, by Timothy Lane, Atish Ghosh, Javier Hamann, Steven Phillips, Marianne Schulze-Ghattas, and Tsidi Tsikata. 1999.

177. Perspectives on Regional Unemployment in Europe, by Paolo Mauro, Eswar Prasad, and Antonio Spilimbergo. 1999.

176. Back to the Future: Postwar Reconstruction and Stabilization in Lebanon, edited by Sena Eken and Thomas Helbling. 1999.

175. Macroeconomic Developments in the Baltics, Russia, and Other Countries of the Former Soviet Union, 1992–97, by Luis M. Valdivieso. 1998.

174. Impact of EMU on Selected Non–European Union Countries, by R. Feldman, K. Nashashibi, R. Nord, P. Allum, D. Desruelle, K. Enders, R. Kahn, and H. Temprano-Arroyo. 1998.

173. The Baltic Countries: From Economic Stabilization to EU Accession, by Julian Berengaut, Augusto Lopez-Claros, Françoise Le Gall, Dennis Jones, Richard Stern, Ann-Margret Westin, Effie Psalida, Pietro Garibaldi. 1998.

172. Capital Account Liberalization: Theoretical and Practical Aspects, by a staff team led by Barry Eichengreen and Michael Mussa, with Giovanni Dell'Ariccia, Enrica Detragiache, Gian Maria Milesi-Ferretti, and Andrew Tweedie. 1998.

171. Monetary Policy in Dollarized Economies, by Tomás Baliño, Adam Bennett, and Eduardo Borensztein. 1998.

170. The West African Economic and Monetary Union: Recent Developments and Policy Issues, by a staff team led by Ernesto Hernández-Catá and comprising Christian A. François, Paul Masson, Pascal Bouvier, Patrick Peroz, Dominique Desruelle, and Athanasios Vamvakidis. 1998.

169. Financial Sector Development in Sub-Saharan African Countries, by Hassanali Mehran, Piero Ugolini, Jean Phillipe Briffaux, George Iden, Tonny Lybek, Stephen Swaray, and Peter Hayward. 1998.

168. Exit Strategies: Policy Options for Countries Seeking Greater Exchange Rate Flexibility, by a staff team led by Barry Eichengreen and Paul Masson with Hugh Bredenkamp, Barry Johnston, Javier Hamann, Esteban Jadresic, and Inci Ötker. 1998.

167. Exchange Rate Assessment: Extensions of the Macroeconomic Balance Approach, edited by Peter Isard and Hamid Faruqee. 1998

166. Hedge Funds and Financial Market Dynamics, by a staff team led by Barry Eichengreen and Donald Mathieson with Bankim Chadha, Anne Jansen, Laura Kodres, and Sunil Sharma. 1998.

165. Algeria: Stabilization and Transition to the Market, by Karim Nashashibi, Patricia Alonso-Gamo, Stefania Bazzoni, Alain Féler, Nicole Laframboise, and Sebastian Paris Horvitz. 1998.

164. MULTIMOD Mark III: The Core Dynamic and Steady-State Model, by Douglas Laxton, Peter Isard, Hamid Faruqee, Eswar Prasad, and Bart Turtelboom. 1998.

163. Egypt: Beyond Stabilization, Toward a Dynamic Market Economy, by a staff team led by Howard Handy. 1998.

162. Fiscal Policy Rules, by George Kopits and Steven Symansky. 1998.

161. The Nordic Banking Crises: Pitfalls in Financial Liberalization? by Burkhard Dress and Ceyla Pazarbaşıoğlu. 1998.

160. Fiscal Reform in Low-Income Countries: Experience Under IMF-Supported Programs, by a staff team led by George T. Abed and comprising Liam Ebrill, Sanjeev Gupta, Benedict Clements, Ronald McMorran, Anthony Pellechio, Jerald Schiff, and Marijn Verhoeven. 1998.

159. Hungary: Economic Policies for Sustainable Growth, Carlo Cottarelli, Thomas Krueger, Reza Moghadam, Perry Perone, Edgardo Ruggiero, and Rachel van Elkan. 1998.

158. Transparency in Government Operations, by George Kopits and Jon Craig. 1998.

157. Central Bank Reforms in the Baltics, Russia, and the Other Countries of the Former Soviet Union, by a staff team led by Malcolm Knight and comprising Susana Almuiña, John Dalton, Inci Otker, Ceyla Pazarbaşıoğlu, Arne B. Petersen, Peter Quirk, Nicholas M. Roberts, Gabriel Sensenbrenner, and Jan Willem van der Vossen. 1997.

156. The ESAF at Ten Years: Economic Adjustment and Reform in Low-Income Countries, by the staff of the International Monetary Fund. 1997.

155. Fiscal Policy Issues During the Transition in Russia, by Augusto Lopez-Claros and Sergei V. Alexashenko. 1998.

154. Credibility Without Rules? Monetary Frameworks in the Post–Bretton Woods Era, by Carlo Cottarelli and Curzio Giannini. 1997.

153. Pension Regimes and Saving, by G.A. Mackenzie, Philip Gerson, and Alfredo Cuevas. 1997.

152. Hong Kong, China: Growth, Structural Change, and Economic Stability During the Transition, by John Dodsworth and Dubravko Mihaljek. 1997.

151. Currency Board Arrangements: Issues and Experiences, by a staff team led by Tomás J.T. Baliño and Charles Enoch. 1997.

150. Kuwait: From Reconstruction to Accumulation for Future Generations, by Nigel Andrew Chalk, Mohamed A. El-Erian, Susan J. Fennell, Alexei P. Kireyev, and John F. Wilson. 1997.

149. The Composition of Fiscal Adjustment and Growth: Lessons from Fiscal Reforms in Eight Economies, by G.A. Mackenzie, David W.H. Orsmond, and Philip R. Gerson. 1997.

148. Nigeria: Experience with Structural Adjustment, by Gary Moser, Scott Rogers, and Reinold van Til, with Robin Kibuka and Inutu Lukonga. 1997.

Note: For information on the title and availability of Occasional Papers not listed, please consult the IMF Publications Catalog or contact IMF Publication Services.